# JOB INTERVIEW

Top Notch Tips and Tricks to Succeed in Any Job Interview

(Learn How to Job Interview and Master the Key Interview Skills!)

**Jeffrey Phillips**

Published by John Kembrey

## **Jeffrey Phillips**

All Rights Reserved

*Job Interview: Top Notch Tips and Tricks to Succeed in Any Job Interview (Learn How to Job Interview and Master the Key Interview Skills!)*

ISBN 978-1-77485-236-1

All rights reserved. No part of this guide may be reproduced in any form without permission in writing from the publisher except in the case of brief quotations embodied in critical articles or reviews.

Legal & Disclaimer

The information contained in this book is not designed to replace or take the place of any form of medicine or professional medical advice. The information in this book has been provided for educational and entertainment purposes only.

The information contained in this book has been compiled from sources deemed reliable, and it is accurate to the best of the Author's knowledge; however, the Author cannot guarantee its accuracy and validity and cannot be held liable for any errors or omissions. Changes are periodically made to this book. You must consult your doctor or get professional medical advice before using any of the suggested remedies, techniques, or information in this book.

Upon using the information contained in this book, you agree to hold harmless the Author from and against any damages, costs, and expenses, including any legal fees potentially resulting from the application of any of the information provided by this guide. This disclaimer applies to any damages or injury caused by the use and application, whether directly or indirectly, of any advice or information presented, whether for breach of contract, tort, negligence, personal injury, criminal intent, or under any other cause of action.

You agree to accept all risks of using the information presented inside this book. You need to consult a professional medical practitioner in order to ensure you are both able and healthy enough to participate in this program.

## Table of Contents

**INTRODUCTION** ............................................................... 1

**CHAPTER 1: BASICS OF A STAR BEHAVIORAL INTERVIEW** .. 3

**CHAPTER 2: WHY SHOULD WE EMPLOY YOU?** ................. 28

**CHAPTER 3: FACE TO FACE INTERVIEWS FACE TO FACE INTERVIEW** ...................................................................... 35

**CHAPTER 4: JOB INTERVIEW BASICS** ................................ 51

**CHAPTER 5: AT THE TIME OF THE INTERVIEW, LOOK FOR A MEMOIR** .......................................................................... 57

**CHAPTER 6: WHAT ARE YOU WEARING?** ......................... 73

**CHAPTER 7: FINDING THE RIGHT JOB** ............................... 77

**CHAPTER 8: THE RESUME** ................................................ 81

**CHAPTER 9: INTERVIEW QUESTIONS AND ANSWER** ........ 88

**CHAPTER 10: EXAMPLES OF PROFESSIONAL THEMES** .... 100

**CHAPTER 11: WHAT'S HOLDING YOUR INTERVIEW SUCCESS BACK? REVIEWING WHICH THOUGHTS DO THE DAMAGE** ........................................................................ 104

**CHAPTER 12: "DESCRIBE YOURSELF IN ONE WORD."** ..... 110

CHAPTER 13: THE INTERVIEW BEHAVIOUR..................... 121

CHAPTER 14: DIFFERENT TYPES OF INTERVIEWS ........... 128

CHAPTER 15: WHY SHOULD WE HIRE YOU?................... 145

CHAPTER 16: HIGH QUALITIES RESPECTED BY EMPLOYERS ................................................................................ 152

CHAPTER 17: WHAT'S THE POINT OF THIS JOB?............. 174

CONCLUSION................................................................ 184

# Introduction

Interviews provide the opportunity to display your abilities as well as your knowledge, experiences, and even your personality. Most of us are from having to undergo interviews at least once in our professional careers. We all go through more than others, and we all hate these, yet we all look forward to these events with a degree of anxiety and fear. They don't need to be terrifying however, they can be.

Your Mind's Frame

In my own experience, the best way to start conducting the interview process is to constantly be reminded of what you can do to help the company - and put yourself in the right mindset.

The mindset that you must have prior to attending an interview should be one where your mind is focused on what you are able to contribute to, and provide for the company.

Look at the best way to ease the burden of your company What skills, knowledge of experience, personality and expertise do you have that can help?

Interviewers are looking to talk with candidates and find applicants who view things in terms of how an employee can contribute to the organization, not just what the organization can provide the employee.

## Chapter 1: Basics of A Star Behavioral Interview

Interviews with a behavioral component are being taken into consideration by many businesses. The questions you are asked to answer will require an impressive demonstration of your abilities and experience related to the job you are applying for, in contrast to the typical job interview questions that only require you to describe the things you have done in your character or to discuss your experiences. You must be able to see that questions are generally structured by presenting a scenario that asks you about the action you've taken to respond to similar situations previously and what the result was.

The interviewer will want to know how you'll handle the situation and you'll have to respond with a clear explanation of the actions you took. The primary goal of this is to demonstrate that your past successes have a positive influence on your future success in the future. You don't necessarily need to be able to recall your answers in your head or even have a clear picture of the experiences you'd like to talk about and share your experiences in your interview.

Explain to the interviewer the ways you've been working efficiently under pressure.

If the interviewer is considering offering you a job that is extremely stressful is likely to be interested in knowing how well you can perform under stress. You need to be able give real examples to demonstrate your previous experiences under anxiety and the way you managed the circumstances.

How do you deal with problems and an example

However, despite your position there could be some problems, and it might not be normal. If such issues arise in the course of the interview, the person who is conducting the interview will require you to describe what you'll do when you encounter awkward situations. It is important to focus on how you handled an issue that provoked your thoughts when you answer.

Do you make mistakes What do you do to manage these?

There is no perfect candidate and we all are likely to make a mistake or two at the time. The manager who is hiring you will be interested in knowing what you did in the event of a mishap.

How do you establish your goals

The interviewer is very interested in the way you formulate your ideas and establish the goals you be aiming to achieve. You can easily go through this process by sharing instances that you have had or witnessed regarding the success of goal setting.

Be sure to discuss the goals you've achieved and the way you achieved them.

The interviewer will take an interest in finding out know what you are doing to help you to reach your goals and what actions you follow to help you to achieve these goals.

Examples of how you collaborated in a group

Many jobs require you to be part of a group. The interviewer or hiring manager will want you to be aware of how to conduct yourself in a group and how you interact with other team members in your vicinity and those whom you collaborate with.

What makes a Behavioral Interview True?

The most well-known interview questions that you'll always go through are the questions based on behavior. It is inevitable to encounter these kinds of questions whenever you are in an interview, regardless of the type of company you are talking to. You must understand how to handle them and understand what they are. Here are a few aspects that will help you to navigate through. There are certain elements of the

STAR concept that are discussed in the following paragraphs.

*Situation*

As the first part, will require you to understand the context in which you respond. You should make use of this as the basis for you to explain the details of the kind of scenarios you'd like to learn more deeply about.

*Task*

This is the second element of the STAR method It will be about the impact you made within the environment. The component won't want to analyze the things you did, however it is looking at what you can expect in this scenario.

*Action*

It is important to move to the next stage by describing the tasks you're required to complete in order to address the problem. This part will put the attention on specific actions as well as the motivations behind the steps. The focus is on what took place in the true sense, and not what could have happened.

Results

This is the final component of the STAR method and it is the one that will need to know the result of each aspect all things considered. It will place all its attention on the more intricate specifics of the problem and will try to figure out the actions taken in the past factors that led to this particular result.

The most frequently asked questions in a Behavioral interview

In the event that you have an organization of employees who are working on a particular task which is common to them all in your workplace as an employer, you should know how your employees react to various situations. Being a successful employee, it's not just about being able to fulfill a job technically but also be able to deal with the scenarios that may be encountered during the course of your job. Here are some most frequently asked questions about behavior:

* You'll need to discuss occasions when you were working closely with someone who had a different personality than your own.

* You'll be required to discuss a circumstance you would like to be been handled differently with your colleague.

* You must provide an example of times that you did not match the expectations of your clients. What was the situation and what did you do to rectify the issue?

1. What's your top priorities?

* Would you be capable of describing instances where you either failed or did well? What was your response to the circumstances?

Tell us about your biggest accomplishment?

What are the strategies that can help you keep yourself motivated?

* Have you had the courage to deal with any conflict? If so and what were your strategies?

* Can you provide an example of the time you tried to convince anyone?

* How do you approach your duties?

The behavioral questions you're asked about will result in the most fundamental things, like:

• Strategies to manage certain situations

* Your thinking skills

* Your comparison to other candidates

These elements allow for the interviewer to get to know your character as a candidate. The interviewer will inquire in to the personality of you and talents that you can bring to the job and the skills you possess to fulfill the job you've been assigned. The manager who is hiring you will want to know certain aspects of your character when they inquire about you to answer questions regarding your behavior. In the beginning, they'll be looking to find out the way you behaved prior to the actual situations you face. This is crucial since the questions aren't just about imaginary situations. the manager who is hiring you doesn't want to know how the applicant will act, all they're interested in was how you behaved.

In addition, the questions will want to understand and comprehend the value you have contributed to the actual scenario. Interviewers wants to know what you did and what were the factors that helped determine the outcomes. It's not just about what someone else did an organization, group or individual did, or even something that somebody else has done the interviewer wants to know your behavior and character traits and how they influence on the circumstances. The manager who is hiring you will want to know more about your style and actions and the actions that you did to impress your boss.

In the end, the hiring manager needs to understand how you'll determine and analyze different workplace situations. This gives them an opportunity to make an understanding of your abilities compared to other applicants, and help them in assessing your abilities that is compatible with the workplace. This means that you need to be able define the terms success, failure or a mistake. The hiring manager isn't seeking to hear from you about them the exact procedures and actions you chose to do. Their primary concerns are in the scenario you describe as be an experiment. A lot of people consider the unique circumstances at work as trials.

Tips on how to Prepare for Behavioral Interviews using the STAR

There are a variety of ways you can start with STAR and it will work to your advantage and you can gain its grasp through:

* Understanding the concept behind the STAR

* Reasons for why the questions you're being asked to answer behavioral questions

* Methods by which STAR can assist you to address the inquiries

Simple steps can assist you prepare for behavioral questions using STAR

Make a list of your abilities and experience

Start by creating a list of all your capabilities and previous experiences. They will assist you in determining whether you be able to provide a great and necessary performance and will help you to know the job you've succeeded in achieving after making an application for. It's not only about listing your skills and qualifications you possess as you possess a variety of them. The most important thing is to focus on the fundamental skills you require for a particular job. To find out what these are, you should look through the job posting. You must be able be able to comprehend it and and highlight any skills and experience which are listed by the employer and record them in an outline. You may write down a number of them or just a few as you are required. The most important thing is to acquire the essential competencies that will aid you in your role and the specific task setting. It is also possible to take in consideration other abilities that your employer hasn't stated, but you are aware that they could be helpful. They could be connected to the skills that the employer has mentioned as well as the skills you already have.

Pick a moment in which you demonstrate your skills or knowledge

You have the abilities listed. You are aware of what an employers are looking for and what your answers must have an impact on. Lastly, you must demonstrate the capabilities by demonstrating them. The next move you're doing is to match every skill with a real-life scenario. It is essential to find the SITUATION within the STAR. You should decide from what you've done and dealt with at a certain moment, and are able to do. You must provide the context of your abilities and appearances. It is best if you can provide examples of situations that are identical to those you're expected to handle in your new job. Note the functions of the STAR

Now you need to pull the STAR template and go through each one of them, and give them a the STAR treatment. A few templates can aid you with filling in any important details that you encounter. The models' questions are a good guideline when you need to write a response. Once you reach this point, you are able to write something similar to an answer you are able to offer. You are permitted to use examples of questions that are typical questions that require a response. What you need to learn is how to show off your capabilities and make use of real examples to illustrate your responses. Additionally, you must learn your STAR strategy.

There are several examples of interview behavior questions as well as STAR responses. To ensure you have the best experiencepossible, you must get some ideas for how to analyze several examples. Certain fundamental behavioral questions are frequently asked during job interviews. It is possible to learn the various instances of responses or responses that have been uncovered in using the STAR strategy. It is expected to speak about times when you were the leader and the actions you took. Have you ever had the chance to commit mistakes? How did you overcome it? Give the hiring manager one example of a plan you've worked on and the way you managed to accomplish it.

If you are able to use the STAR method, you'll be able to become the center of attention in your job interview that you've been through. The behavioral questions will help you since they're an essential aspect in the interview. They are used to assess you attentively, and you will be able to assess your position within the company. They will be able to tell the manager you are, and what it is that you've done in order to help them make predictions regarding your experiences within the position. If you're looking to answer the questions, the most effective method is the STAR method. It helps you to highlight the correct elements of your performance in the past and will provide your answers with the correct structure and quality.

The most efficient way to answer questions about your behavior is using the STAR method. It can be a well-organized way to formulate an answer. STAR is also a synonym for situation, task, action and Results. The STAR matrix is an odd method you can utilize to prepare for interviews. It also explains how to allow you to download it as a part of this course. If you wish to get the most out of the interview based on behavior, you need to be prepared. What is going to kill the benefits in the STAR matrix is that it requires you to reflect on your own experiences. If you finish the matrix, you will store the information into the short term memory of your brain. When you are faced with questions that are based on behavioral analysis, you'll have your answer that you can present to the interviewer.

Some tips can aid you with the STAR matrix in the following manner:

Situations

It could represent your initial job and you don't need to worry about it because everyone else has beginning to find a place. The requirements you are required to meet shouldn't affect your work. If you need to pick a specific situation that is not yours, you'll need to consider a variety of options when it is possible. If you're still fresh to the field, it is likely that you will use the stories of your work, school experiences as well as freestyle activities.

Tasks

It is important to keep your tasks brief and simple. You will need to be aware of your part in the scenario and also how the character came to be your concern or your situation, in the first place.

Actions

The steps you should take in an incident. The potential employer will place the focus on how you manage stressful situations that you encounter. What are the steps you've taken to resolve the issue? There are a few traits employers look for when evaluating prospective employees:

• Initiatives - What can future employees know the existence of an issue in the first place?

* Approach - What's the strategy you are using in dealing with the issue? Are you able make choices about how to tackle the situation immediately? Or do you must collect opinions and data about how to proceed?

* Setting Goals - Before you take the first steps Are you thinking about what the end result will be like?

If you're discussing your actions, think that you are putting your best foot forward. It is important to think about what you would like and someone who feels comfortable working with or with you.

Results

They are a crucial component that is a crucial part of STAR framework. You may decide to frame the ideal situation and then try to explain how easy your actions are and what they are. It is important whether you don't concentrate on the results. It is important to describe the outcomes that you've achieved against the context in which you began. Certain tips will help you communicate your accomplishments in an interview.

* You may compare your results into the financial impact if you are a revenue-generating portion of a sales-like business. Focus on the revenue generated, business that has been won, as well as the value that will be accrued by the clients you have added.

Focus on the time savings that can be beneficial to your team when you've just implemented a brand new analysis or report.

Always keep in mind that the primary goal is to display an impressive track record in order for the manager who is hiring to allow you to be hired. You must link your past achievements with the questions you're tackling to answer. With this in mind, be aware that success in an interview isn't an accident of fate. If you're determined to follow the steps to complete your STAR matrix and conduct the ability to review your responses and your responses, you could be successful on situations where you have to conduct a behavioral interview. There are some important lessons to take away for those who want to prepare for a behavior interview for instance:

* Many businesses are inclined to employ a behavior interview to assist in

determining the way employees who are capable can handle situations.

\* If you use the STAR structure, the times when you answer questions, it will aid in making your responses succinct and clearly framed. how you'll be in a position to handle scenarios.

\* You must be aware that it's essential to complete the STAR matrix in order to store your matrix answers in your short-term memory and write the story that your future boss must be able to understand.

A few tutorials can assist you prepare for interviews while you read or look through them. The following are the tutorials:

It is recommended to look through the business instructors and tutorials on the internet. They have great tutorials on how you can answer complex behavioral questions. There is the option of placing them into the STAR matrix and then you can check the results for the specifics of them.

\* You can also find an excellent guidebook on how you can answer the most frequent twenty questions asked in interviews.

2. Cover Letter Your Grand Entrance

One thing that's missing in the plethora of resumes I've seen is an official cover letter. The Cover letter should be your first impression or your main course. It's a chance to provide the prospective employer a glimpse of your character as person. You've put together a powerful professional resume which gives your employer an impression of your professionalism and work experience But this is your opportunity to demonstrate why you are the best candidate or merit the job.

It is important to craft your cover letter with professionalism however, you should also discover an opportunity to distinct from other resumes. While you can locate examples of cover letter templates using the aid of a Google search, you should keep in mind that these templates are so common that anyone can put their details into them and then use the templates. The aim for your letter of cover is to offer employers a glimpse of your character. The cover letter by introducing a favorite quotation that's relevant to the job, or with a claim that is intriguing to the reader. Find a unique method to grab the attention of your reader.

Employers are drawn to the cover letters of offices because they have specific dynamic. If you're applying for an organization that is smaller it's important that your character is compatible with the employees already in the office. I was in a small office with six employees, where everyone was very friendly, however when it came to working and work, everyone was so focused that the office remained relatively quiet. We decided to recruit an individual who had never been in the office. Although her skills for the job were a good fit, we realized that she was an irritable chatterbox. Everyday she would tell personal stories from her home or discuss a work event that she was annoyed or humorous. Although we could be able to listen at her from a completely different space however, the office was just too fast-paced and crowded for us to be able to continue the conversation. Actually the conversation would usually interfere with the urgency that had to be present in the work day. It is vital for businesses to identify the perfect match, so they can take the objectives of the business quickly and effectively. A cover letter could give the little insight that is necessary to assure your employer that you're the perfect match.

Another reason employers want to read a cover note is because it provides the entire hiring process a sense of humanness. It is easy to read resume after resume and be exhausting, but the freshness of a cover letter will bring life to the page. Instead of just looking at a page of words, employers will be able to see reflections of candidates mind.

Be the envy of your friends with your wit

The first time I met him, I took the initiative to research and learn all I could on his specialty which was Motocross. I did research on everything from racing teams to how to create motors for bikes and each time I had new information to give out to surprise him. It worked...we're we are now married.

The same way to impress prospective employers. The cover letter you send to employers should focus on one or two accomplishments the company has achieved or highlight how the company's operations are run. Be sure to show your passion for the companyand not just about the job. Employers want to hire a person who is dedicated to the company and not just seeking the next pay check. Inform them that your goals coincide with the company's goals. Let them know that by choosing you, the business will expand and invest in a prosperous future.

Be Charming

As you put all the necessary elements together for the cover letter you write, finish it off with a little flair. Bring your reader in by your charisma. If you've got a funny humored personality, you can create a piece that will make the reader laugh. If you're blessed with a gentle spirit, appeal to your reader's compassion. Keep your reader in mind and also the fact that the reader will have a lot of resumes and letters to read through. Make sure you convey a wealth of quality into a short amount of words.

# Chapter 2: Why Should We Employ You?

You consider yourself to be very smart, hard-working, multi-talented, the one never who gets tired; always accept a challenge, out-of-the-box-thinker who is ever ready to take on the world. Why do you feel that every time the interviewer asks you a question in an interview - Why Should We Choose You? You suddenly stop talking and start stuttering?

Common Faults

An incorrect answer to a simple question such as this will make a person who isn't prepared for interviewing in danger. Therefore, first we must understand the reason why people ask that question first in the in the first place.

Do you think this is a trick question?

It's not true! They're not trying to make it difficult in any way! They just want to make sure that you've got the skills required to be qualified for the specific job, and that you truly understand what is

required to be a perfect fit to the job and also that you possess the knowledge they're looking for. So, in other words, give them two things that are simple:
You know what they require as well as,
You can give them the things they require.
Glib or flippant reply
A lot of interviewees who aren't all ready for the question generally give ineffective responses such as:
"I believe that I'm a top performer in all that you do. I am confident that I'll give it my the fullest effort and that I'm far better than my competitors. I'm the perfect candidate for this job and, frankly I'm sure that if you decide to hire me you'll make the most intelligent decision of your life since you are able to see the real potential".
Or,
"Umm Well I'm sure I'm clever and I work hard, and I'm capable of completing the tasks I'm being required to do. I'd love to be part of this group and ..."

Buh, bye! It's obvious that you're lost!

Remember that every firm (when they advertise an opening) will have a specific kind of candidate to consider when conducting interviews for the job. The candidate will usually require the specific qualities that the company is adamant about or places an emphasis on.

Answering the question - Why should we choose you?

The question"Why Should We Employ You? This is a great opportunity for you to present your abilities to the interviewer and emphasize that you're the ideal candidate for this job!

This is a question about checking your confidence in yourself. If you're unable to respond quickly and easily, you're giving the interviewer a reason to doubt your self-confidence or capability.

Below are the most effective tips for giving the perfect answer for this query:

Customize Your Reply

Each business has a specific set of characteristics that you must possess in order for success during the interview. It's on you to show that you are able to demonstrate all of these traits. It is possible to do this by tailoring your responses to show how your capabilities and experiences align with the stated criteria.

Study the company where you're applying Research is the only method to comprehend and identify what qualities the business seeks and to highlight them in your answers. You must conduct an extensive amount of research about the company and search for clues! The first clue is typically in the job ad (job summary). The job description typically has a list of qualifications ('required capabilities and skills'), and you are able to emphasize these in your responses. Do your research to find out what's most crucial to the business as well as to the interviewer personally. What are the declared values of the business or the mission statement? What do they believe is worthy enough to highlight in press announcements? What industry awards or recognition has the company won? In acknowledging certain facts about the company you're actually flattering both the company and interviewer by showing that you've taken the time to study them. Don't think that flattery isn't a powerful tool in an interview!

What are the qualities you possess You don't have that your competitors do?

Okay, so you may need to compete with the other job-seekers with similar skills, experiences and expertise. The trick to succeed here is to answer the question with confidence and in a unique way. You must focus on the unique characteristic you possess that can help you get the job and the overall development of the business. What is it that makes you unique?

Make them aware that you're a problem Solver

When you have conducted a thorough study of the business, you can identify a problem or need that has led the company to offer the job (which you're applying for). When you answer this question, emphasize your ability to resolve the specific issue or need that your company is having to address.

Pro Tip - Practice makes perfect!

As there's a high likelihood that you'll be required to answer the question in one manner or other during an interview, it is important to be prepared ahead of time. It's not a good idea to be unprepared, stumble, or make accidental mistakes that could indicate that you're not in confidence.

Follow all of the advice above and develop an exact pitch that is natural. It is important to try it out with a acquaintance, or in the mirror. Make sure to respond in a conversational and informal tone. I recently read an article that suggested you can practice your responses with dogs! The concept was that if one could make use of your voice and pitch to attract the attention of dogs that you'll likely be ahead of the other applicants in a real interview!

## Chapter 3: Face To Face Interviews
## Face To Face Interview

This is the section of the book that discuss some of the questions prospective employers are eager to hear. Remember that our goal is to be remembered by them when they make the final decision to hire. We accomplish this by combining our findings with our experiences and, in doing so, assist the interviewer to visualize us performing the task.

Question:

Why should we choose you?

You can prepare for this by reading the job description. Create a list of specifications for the job that includes skills and qualifications. Create a list of qualities you possess that meet the requirements. For each one, think of a specific moment when you utilized that quality to accomplish something in your work. For instance, if declare that you are an "team member," think of a moment in which the ability you have to function as a part of a team led to the successful completion of a task.

Answer:

You're looking for someone who is competent in managing over 12 employees. Through my experiences, I've built a strong team-building and motivational abilities. I was awarded manager of the year due to my methods of encouraging employees to achieve the quarterly targets and even exceed them. If hired, I'll provide my leadership capabilities and strategies to achieve profitable results to this job.

Or

The job description declare that you are looking for an assistant teacher who has compassion and patience. As an instructor at a summer camp

schools for children over the last two years. I've developed my capacity to be extremely patient while making academic progress in my class. The experience of teaching reading to children aged 6-18 has taught me methods to work with students of all age groups and abilities all the while keeping a smile on their face. My previous employer frequently placed me in the classrooms of students with the most severe disabilities in learning because of my record of accomplishment. I'll bring not just expertise, but also patience, and innovative problem-solving skills to the position.

Or

I believe I'm an ideal candidate for this job. My MBA degree and more than 10 years of experience in managing hundreds of employees and providing training, has allowed me to boost productivity and decrease employee turnover. I am convinced that I can achieve the same feat for your business and make a fantastic partner to your team.

Question:

Tell me more about you?

It's a very common interview question that I find it a bit surprising that applicants don't take the time to plan the exact way to answer it. This could be due to the fact that the questions are so unsettling and casual that we let down our guard and go into the mode of rambling. Be sure to not lose your cool in any way in the process of interviewing. Remember that they don't require to have a 20-minute discussion about your life's journey. It is important to provide them with a an answer in a matter of 1-2 minutes.

Answer:

I'm a well-established Manager thanks to my training and development programs have led to the reduction of revenue of more than $5 million in the case of (XYZ company) in my tenure working with them.

Question:

What is the best way to measure success?

Answer:

I have seen success in a variety of ways. In my work, it's fulfilling the objectives established by the company the supervisors, my colleagues and me employees. My understanding is that based on my research that your business is recognized for not just rewarding achievement, but also giving employees the chance to develop also. In my spare time, I like playing sports. My success on the field is the winning move.

Or

It's about working hard and doing my job effectively. I'm being recognized as someone who does the best job and strives best to achieve their goals.

Or

Success is not just my own work but also on the efforts that my colleagues do. To think of myself as successful, the team has to accomplish both the individual and team objectives.

Question:

What kind of work environment are you most comfortable with?

Make sure that you're flexible since, at this point in the interview process you aren't sure what it will be like working for the business.

Answer:

In my work environment , I can be very flexible. What would you say about the working environment?

Question:

What are the reasons you would like to join us?

Answer:

This job is an ideal match for my experience and skills and includes (state these abilities). As I mentioned earlier in my previous job, I had (restate achievements).

Or

According to your website, you have plans to open 10 more stores within the next year and I'd like to join an expanding company.

Question:

Why would you like to quit your job?

In the first place, absolutely not allowed to speak negatively about your boss, former employer. This can always create the interviewer in doubt minds of "will they be blaming me or my company when they quit?"

Answer:

There's not enough room for advancement in my current company and I'm eager to take on an opportunity.

Or

I'm in search of a more challenging challenge and to expand my career , but I can't work part time and find a job when I was working. It was not appropriate to make use of my ex-colleague's time.

Or

I'm moving to the area due to family issues and I quit my previous job to make the move.

Or

I recently graduated from college and would like to use my academic background for my next job.

Or

There's not enough room for advancement at my current job and I'm eager to start an opportunity.

Question:

What can you expect from a manager?

Answer:

I'd prefer to talk to my supervisor about an issue or thought and be comfortable to share my thoughts. I would also like that my boss to be honest and truthful with me, and to inform me what I could improve my job.

Or

I love it when managers don't display favoritism, and they are aware of the needs of their employees and strengths. Naturally, such aspects require time to learn however, I would like my boss to get to know me in this manner.

Question:

What are your weak points?

This is the perfect chance to promote yourself instead of focusing on the things that are wrong with you. Change this question that could be negative into an opportunity to be positive.

Answer:

Being organized wasn't one of my strengths however, I did implement a time management program that helped me to manage my schedule and ensured that prioritised tasks were completed. This way, I realized that I was able to get more time during the day instead of less , and had more productivity because of it.

Or

Sometimes, I struggle to delegate tasks to other people. It's sometimes backfired as I'd find myself having much more to do than I was able to take on. I've taken classes on time management and have learned how to delegate more effectively. I'm pleased to report that the last few team projects were a complete achievement.

Question:

Your strengths?

Answer:

I am extremely organized and time management skills, however my strongest strength lies in my ability to efficiently manage many projects and deadlines.

Or

My strengths lie in my flexibility to adapt to changes. As a frontline manager at my last position I was able transform a negative work environment, and create a efficient and supportive team.

Question:

How do you manage pressure, stress or tension?

Answer:

By prioritizing my duties so that I can have an idea of what must be accomplished and I can accomplish it, I can be organized, I reduce any pressure

Question:

What is it that motivates you?

They're just trying to figure out what is essential to success on the work. There isn't a one right or wrong solution, but you must ensure you've sold your expertise.

Answer:

I was the responsible person for numerous projects, where I directed teams of development and introduced new processes that were structured. Teams achieved 100% efficiency, met their deadlines and goals. I was inspired by the task of completing the project before schedule and within budget, as well as by controlling the teams that achieved their goals and goals.

Or

I've always been driven by the pressure of meeting a deadline. during my previous position in which I was accountable for an 85 percent success rate of delivering our product in time and on budget. I'm aware that this job is extremely fast-paced and deadline-driven, so I'm up to the task. Actually I thrive in it.

Question:

How do you work across departments?

Answer:

I can alter and adapt to my surroundings within a matter of seconds, because I
I've worked in different departments throughout my career. My understanding of every department's requirements allows me to accurately transmit details. Shorter communications through email, phone and in person alleviates any frustration and gives me more the flexibility to delegate or complete more challenging tasks.

Question:

What lessons have you gleaned from your mistakes?

Answer:

In the end I've discovered success is a result of having had to fail multiple times, however, what defines them as fail is not quitting. Failure that isn't quit is an element of a system of character development.

Question:

If I had to reach your former employer what would he have to say regarding your decision-making capabilities?

Answer:

He wrote my recommendation letter that specifically outlines my ability to make decisions. They include buying, price control the hiring process, managing time, as well as prospecting.

Question:

How do you feel about your former boss?

Answer:

My previous boss taught me the importance of managing time and was extremely punctual. His uncompromising approach to work pushed me to be more productive and complete deadlines I had never believed were achievable.

Question:

What do you think of yourself 5 years from now?

The interviewer would like to know whether the candidate is ambitious, career-focused and determined to build a successful future in the business.

Answer:

I'd like to gain greater knowledge of the industry. In addition, I enjoy working with other people. In the end, I'd love to hold some kind of management position at this business, in which I'm able to make use of my interpersonal expertise and know-how to benefit those employed by me, and the entire company.

Question:

What are you looking for?

Answer:

I'm more concerned about the job itself rather than the salary. However, I'd like to receive a salary that is within the level for this job in light of my experience of five years. Also, I think a fair pay would take into account the costs to live in the particular area.

Or

I'll need more details regarding the job and its duties before we can discuss the salary, however it would be helpful for you to give me an estimate of the range of salary you've set for this job.

Question:

Do you have a reason for the difference in your job?

Answer:

My work is extremely important for me, which is why I'm not content with just any job. Instead of jumping at any opportunity that is offered to me I'm slow and cautious to ensure that my next position is the one I want to be in.

Question:

What were you most unhappy about at your previous job?

Answer:

It was not something about my previous job that I disliked However, there were some aspects I did not like more than other people. My previous job required me to travel every month at least twice. Although I love to travel, two times per month can be exhausting and I didn't enjoy spending long hours out of the office. I'm pleased to learn that this job requires the least amount of traveling.

Question:

What do your coworkers think of you?

Answer:

My coworkers, in particular (name of the co-worker) always told me my name was "the toughest person they've ever worked with.

Question:

Have you ever experienced disagreements with your boss or colleague? What did you do?

Answer:

I believe that every person at some point had conflicts at work, whether with a boss or a coworker. I've noticed that when confronted with a challenging situation, it's helpful to talk to another person to gain an understanding of the perspective of each person and find a solution that is collaborative whenever it is possible.

## Chapter 4: Job Interview Basics

Interviews for jobs are marked by formality, professionalism, as well as the fear factor, which is the reason some people are not fond of the process. While everyone is looking to land a great job with a reputable company conducting an interview isn't easy due to the uncertainty of interviews as well as the pressure they place on the candidate prior to the date and time for the interview. However, this doesn't mean it is impossible to have a smooth interview experience however. In fact, interviews can be extremely engaging, informative and effortless if you know exactly how to conduct yourself in every moment. If you're prepared it is easy to impress your interviewer and that puts you in the best position to land the job.

Your attitude during a job interview could make a amount of difference and help ensure that you get through the whole procedure. Interviews are basically an opportunity for you to have a one-on-one conversation with potential employers and, as such, you must be focused on what they can provide to the company and the benefits you will profit from the company.

Types of job interview

There are various types of job interview that are available and include the following:

Screening interviews are intended to narrow the pool of applicants. Some applicants do not actually know they're being scrutinized, and at sometimes the screening takes place in person or on the phone. Interviews like these are typical at fairs for career seekers.

The Sequential Interviews: These are interviews in which the candidate will be able to meet multiple interviewers at the same time within the same organization. These types of interviews are frequent and are designed to make sure that the perfect candidate is found by the conclusion of the interview. The best advice for this type or interview is to approach each interviewer like the first interviewer, in order so that you appear constant throughout.

Telephone or electronic interviews Interviews are conducted by phone or electronically like the name suggests. These types of interviews can be difficult because the person being interviewed may not treat the time to consider them with the seriousness they are entitled to. But, you could alter the outcome by treating the interview in the same manner you would conduct an interview face-to-face. If you have when and where the meeting will take place, you should prepare yourself beforehand and have all the information you'll need for the interview on hand to ensure the interview is successful.

Panel interviews These are the kinds of interview where the candidate is in front of a panel or set of interviewers. In these types of interviews, more than one interviewee may be being interviewed simultaneously. They aren't very common in the present, but there are some organizations who prefer interviewing candidates this way.

What do interviewers look for in an interview?

A typical interviewer will pose a set of questions to determine specific abilities and qualities they would like to they are looking to recruit in their organization. So, you need to be careful about how you respond to every question they ask. The topics range from educational background, career goals, and work experience. Here are a few topics they are interested in:

They're looking to gauge your confidence and find out the extent to which you can take it without appearing overly confident. The objective is to see your ability to collaborate with others like you're their peers, but you're just starting out as a novice.

Interviewers are likely to be impressed by your enthusiasm. It is important to show them that you are worthy of the opportunity without appearing desperate. They must also be able to see your willingness to work and the way you would can be a good fit for the position.

Interviews are intended to reveal your potential for success. This is why it's important to describe the steps you've taken and what you've accomplished, as well as the way you're influenced by your thinking process.

Interviewers will want to know your reasoning. This can be seen in how you think about the information you are given.

They will also test your levels of communication, how well you interact with others, and how you interact to others in a workplace.

Interviews are a way to show off your organizational abilities and also. This is evident in how you dress for the event, the way you manage and conduct your self, and how you deal with your belongings that you take along in the interview room.

Things to keep in mind always

Interviewees should be aware that every question in an interview is a part of the process, so you must answer each question carefully and in a thoughtful manner.

There are tricks that can be uncovered during an interview, so be aware not to be fooled by them.

## Chapter 5: At the time of the Interview, Look For A Memoir

If you are interviewing at the workplace of your interviewer there's an excellent strategy that you can employ to start the conversation. As you walk into the office, take a quick look at the wall. Do you see family pictures or other pictures related to hobbies hanging on the walls? What kinds of keepsakes are displayed on their desks and shelves? Are there inspirational quotes displayed? Fun sayings? Star Wars figures? What do you know about the interviewer from their work place?

Look for something (if you are able to) that you share to share with the interviewer, and begin your conversation by mentioning it. As an example, suppose you are a skydiver and see an image of the person you are interviewing skydiving. It is possible to begin by asking: "How many times have you skydived? I've been there and I am eager to try this once more." This can aid in building a rapport with the person you are interviewing which can boost your chances of securing the job. The hiring managers usually select people they like and feel can be considered to fit into the organization. Keep the conversation going for 5-10 minutes, and then you will be able to hear the signal when it's time to begin the interview. At the time, you'll need to begin selling yourself.

I conducted a series of four consecutive interviews during my office trip. I found a memento at every office and began the conversation in this manner. In one interview we would never stop talking over the souvenir (football). Even though our teams of choice were big rivals, I made sure to keep conversations going smoothly and eventually received the chance to win.

Bring the energy

If the interview is not early in the morning It's difficult to know the presence of other interviewees before the interviewer when you sit together with an interviewer.

There's a possibility that the interviewer is exhausted after conducting multiple interviews in succession.

Research has shown that the initial five minutes of an interview are crucial to making an impression. A positive and enthusiastic candidate stands out from the rest and makes an impression with the interviewer.

Before the interview starts You should:

1.) Smile when you greet the interviewer.

2.) Hold out your hand and shake their hands (not too hard, but also not overly soft) as you look at them in the eyes as you introduce yourself.

3.) After the greetings are over, lean slightly toward the left, keep eye contact and display enthusiasm in answering their questions, and asking questions of your questions of your own.

4.) Make use of your hands to back up the examples you present.

5.) Mirror the body language of the interviewer (this is known as mirroring) to make them feel at relaxed.

6) Show confidence and positivity by your body expression.

7) Be sure to breathe!

Do Not Criticize Your Current Employer

If you're going to interviews because you have an unprofessional boss, do not divulge this in the interview. Don't criticize your current (or previous) boss, your company or colleagues. The main focus of your interview should be what you can offer your prospective employer. Every second you waste on blaming your current employer is an unproductive chance to showcase the talents you have to offer. You don't want the person you interview (who could end up being Your boss) to believe that they will be the ones to be criticized when you accept the job and transfer to a different firm in the future.

Use the General-To-Specific

In simple terms the goal is to convey three points in the interview:

* Your strengths

*Why your expertise is an excellent fit to the job

How you can assist the department or company

No matter what questions the interviewer asks you, your answer must convey at least one of these points. Employ the general-to-specific method. Begin by identifying the skills the interviewer is talking about in your response, then explain that you possess this skill, and provide specific examples of how you used the skill at your job (or previous) job. Here are a few examples:

Example #1

Interviewer: "We're looking for someone to join us and start working immediately as well as get acquainted on the accounting system and get deep into financials. We're extremely busy, so we don't have plenty of time to learn."

You: "I'm a quick learner. This was the same thing that happened when I began my current job. There was such a high level of activity in the office, they had a lack hours to sit and explain how the financials functioned and I was able to get up to speed by asking the staff what they did. I was able to figure it out without any prior knowledge and was able succeed very quickly."

Example #2

Interviewer: "This is a sales job. The most important thing we want to know is how this individual will interact with our current customers. The majority of our sales are to customers who are already in our database, so building and maintaining strong relationships with them is essential."

Your: "I'm all about customer service. A few months later, they placed me as the manager of the most important and lucrative client. I was able to swiftly build a good connection with them. Their sales have increased 15 percent since I took control of the account. I'm able take what I've learned in this case and apply it to customers."

Example 3:

Interviewer: "This department has experienced lots of turnover because of a poor manager who has left recently. It would be a matter of replacing this individual and beginning with a fresh start. There'll be plenty of barriers to repair with the rest of the personnel. It is important to first earn their trust and then encourage them to perform better."

The Customer: "Gaining and keeping the trust of my employees is my top goal. If there is no trust, everything breaks down. This situation reminds me of my previous job with my employer. I was promoted to a different department, and morale was low. It was necessary to remove a few individuals leave, but those who stayed with me eventually came around, and formed a wonderful team."

The same general-to-specific approach is to be employed in the case of an interviewer who wants to probe your experiences. Here are a few examples:

Example #1

Interviewer: "I see here on your resume that you were the project manager of an implementation project for software. Do you have any more information about this?"

Yousay "Yes I'd be delighted to. The experience has helped me enhance my skills in managing projects. I divided the project into a sequence of assignments and deadlines. I gave each project to one team member , and followed their progress toward the deadlines. A lot of coaching was needed to help me develop my management of people skills. It was an amazing experience that is relevant to the project management skills listed in the job description. Do you have any more details regarding this?"

Example #2

Interviewer: "Can you tell me more about the talks you have made in your current job?"

Your: "I really enjoy giving presentations. Every quarter, our team has the responsibility of providing a financial report to the CFO as well as their direct subordinates. This takes a lot of preparation and rehearsal. The presentation I am presenting has an element of the annual forecast, therefore I take the data and translate them in a accessible format by using chart and graphs. I usually spend three hours practicing my presentation, and then I conduct two walkthroughs with my team, where we receive feedback on ways to improve the presentation. I then take the feedback and continue with another half-hour or so of rehearsals. The day before your presentation, I do a few final adjustments and get into the conference room before the scheduled time to make sure that the technology is in place. While presenting, I am able to answer queries from CFO and I respond to my best ability. It generally goes easily. Do you have any information about the kinds of presentations that are expected for this position?"

Example #3

Interviewer: "Can you tell me about a situation where you had to manage an employee who was extremely difficult and how you dealt with the situation?"

Then you: "I have very high expectations for employees who work for me. In the past, an employee was transferred from a different department to my team. I was not involved regarding the transfer, and I was able to tell from the beginning that the person was moved around the company following the acrimonious burning of bridges at each of his places. I set my expectations and clear from the start and he didn't live up to the requirements. He was simply lazy and didn't even care. I met with my boss and requested permission to place him on a plan to improve his performance that we followed through with. Six months later, no improvement, so I removed him from the company. Following that, two of his former managers contacted me and expressed their gratitude for my solving the issue."

Avoid Inappropriate Questions

We hope that this doesn't be the case, but there may be instances where the wrong question is asked regarding your sexual orientation, health or gender, relationships, or even appearance (sexual in the sense of). If it happens, refer the interviewer on your CV and previous experience by declaring: "I'm not sure how this question pertains to my desire for this job However, I'd prefer to keep the conversation about your resume."

If the questioning persists, just end the interview, say thank you to your interviewer and then leave. If you're likely to be working with the person you interview every day it is likely that you will have to deal with a hostile work environment, and that's not going to be a great fit in the first place. Be courteous even if your gesture isn't acknowledged.

Be honest

I hope this is not a problem that you must be completely honest during the interview. It is possible to exaggerate your abilities or work experience However, by doing this, you might create the impression that you have the qualifications that the interviewer is seeking. It could hurt you when you are offered the job. The most important thing you'd like to avoid is to lose work after the employer discovers you've been lying about your experiences during the interview.

Ask Intelligent Questions

You've passed an exhausting interview. You've answered all questions and moved from general to specific in your answers as well as impressed your interviewer by your expertise of the industry and company. The interviewer asks "So are you able to answer any questions you'd like to ask I?" You might be inclined to decline and leave the room when the door opens, but this is a big mistake! Engaging in 3-5 thoughtful questions about the business (including the interviewer's own experience with this company) will benefit you and make a lasting impression.

I came to the conclusion of an interview and the interviewer wanted to know whether he had addressed all of my questions. I seen on the website of the company about a "Global Day of Service' program that sees the business shut down on a specific day of the year and puts all employees to the community to do an entire day of volunteer work. Employees are able to serve anywhere they like. I inquired with the interviewer about what he usually does. He seemed amazed that I had completed my homework. He told me he comes back to the high school he attended to assist in repairs and maintenance which he truly enjoys doing. The sight of old teachers bring back wonderful memories, and is his most favorite holiday of the year. We laughed together as the interview concluded. It was no surprise that I received a job offer (and I accepted it).

Here are some general questions you can ask

"Tell me about your culture of your company."

"How do you feel that you've grown professionally since joining our company?"

"What do you consider to be the most important skill or characteristic required to succeed in this role?"

"What kind of instruction will I receive during those first sixty days?"

"Can you provide me with some idea of the daily responsibilities?"

"What do you find most appealing regarding the firm?"

"Is the business facing any significant challenges in the moment?"

"What is the biggest issue this department has to resolve currently?"

Ask What will happen next?

Once the interview is finished it is perfectly normal to ask for the next step. It will establish expectations and set your mind at peace. The interviewer could be able to say:

"We must conclude all interviews by Friday. Then, we'll meet together as a team to choose the candidates we'd like to invite back for a follow-up interview. It is expected to know whether you've made the cut by Wednesday."

If you require more information Here are some great inquiries:

"What will be your next steps of the process of interviewing?"

"When do I anticipate to hear anything?"

"Is there a specific timeframe for the date when a decision can be taken on this issue?"

Thank the interviewer

When you leave from the space (or your home) take a moment to shake hands of the person you interviewed, look at them in the eye and say thank you to them for taking the time, and for the opportunity to apply for the job. Get an invitation to visit their business. If you're looking to pursue the job be sure to convey this in a brief, clear manner. These are few examples of how to do it:

"This is a wonderful location to work from."

"I'm eagerly anticipating the next stage of this process."

"It's been an honor to have had the pleasure of speaking with you. I'm looking forward to hearing from you in the near future."

"This seems like a fantastic chance to take advantage of it. Take advantage of the rest of your day."

## Chapter 6: What are You Wearing?

Your attire isn't used when you are interviewing, but they could draw attention when you don't take your time to think about it. If you're interviewing for a job which doesn't typically need a suit, it is acceptable to dress in business casual with a good pair of slacks and appropriate shirt. A lot of companies are accepting formal business attire nowadays, so think about this alternative. The most important thing here is to wear a dress that isn't attracting the wrong kind of interest.

I've seen a candidate who showed up wearing sandals, shorts as well as a worn-out t-shirt. In an effort to be innovative and patient, I interviewed the candidate anyway, and was impressed by his background and experiences he listed by his résumé. He was an interesting person however, he did appear as a bit arrogant in the interview. Perhaps he was feeling nervous tension? Add that to his attire led me to believe that he'd be difficult to integrate with my colleagues. I decided not to take him seriously as a candidate. The choice of his dress made the choice about him.

If you decide for a suit,, by absolutely ironing the shirt. A shirt that has wrinkles suggests you're not paying attention to the smallest of details, something that many jobs demand. Check to see if it doesn't contain any stains. If you're wearing a tie, make sure to secure the top button, too. If your collar isn't fitting, consider taking off the top button and sewing it back slightly further away from the edges of your collar. It will not be noticed by anyone and you'll feel more relaxed. More important, you will be have the ability to breathe!

If you can when wearing a tie make sure you wear a long-sleeved t-shirt. In terms of tie, make sure that the tie you wear is) clean,) color-coordinated and) not too long. A tie that is too small will be a bit higher than your beltline. The end of an appropriately tied tie will end at midsection of the belt when standing straight. Make sure you get the right tie. The internet is filled with videos and information regarding this subject. If you're not sure the proper way to tie your tie get someone to assist. Do not delay until the very last minute to resolve this.

Pants are the next item to be considered. If they're dress slacks, make sure you iron them when they're wrinkled or have an attractive crease. If you are wearing jeans, make sure they're fresh and do not have any holes or stains. Stay clear of shorts and sweatpants. Also, shoes. While some individuals go way too far with the shine of their shoes and hygiene I've never paid much to it in my interviews. But, it doesn't harm to dress in shoes that are appropriate to the outfit you're on. Dress shirts, slacks and tie will be noticed if you were wearing running shoes. Begin to prepare the clothes you'll wear for the interview. Make sure you are aware of this simple but vital statement you'll be making.

## Chapter 7: Finding The Right Job

In this section we'll examine how to locate an opportunity that is specifically designed to match your talents and personal style. It is vital to choose the perfect job or else you'll be more likely to become bored and fail to achieve the results you want from your work.

Choose a position that is interesting to you The first step is to choose a job that matches your personality and skills. Do not look for pay checks that are too high if you aren't certain you'd want to do these jobs. The ability to do work is different from being able to think about it. If you're not a person who enjoys perform a routine desk job, you shouldn't be applying for jobs. Look for jobs that challenge you to think outside of the simple box.

Skills sets

Employers always look forward to hiring candidates with the basic skills. A few of them are: the ability to think critically, communicate technical accuracy, and interpersonal capabilities. Logical thinking refers to the capacity of our minds to make decisions and make decisions based on the ability of reasoning. Inductive reasoning, deductive and adductive capabilities are a part of a basic logic set. There are many who are incapable to think logically in difficult situations or in unexpected circumstances. The more reasoning a person has more likely he is of being hired.

Communication

Communication skills are essential to be successful in at work. If you're not able to communicate your concerns to your employer and colleagues in a manner that is convenient for them and efficiently, then you're probably not the best candidate to be working with. A relationship between an employee and employer requires the disclosure of specific actions for the employers. Not telling the employer about the activities or not letting him know about an the important facts that could impact the company's performance is a as a lack of communication skills.

Technical Know-how

The ability to be technically accurate is a important necessity. You could be a wonderful people person. You might possess an I.Q of 130 or more, however if you aren't making the right proper bolts and nuts you will be cut right from the start. Being technically proficient requires you to make your foundations solid. For instance, a job in a bank might require being an expert in maths and accounting. A law firm might require you to be acquainted with the laws of your state and the federal constitution. Therefore, make sure you know the basic knowledge of the technical aspects prior to deciding on a particular job.

Team Work

The job isn't just being a job that is just about receiving a salary. It also has an office with many other employees working with you. It is a rule of thumb to be a worker not only with your employer but with your colleagues. Make sure you're well-equipped to work with colleagues towards the same goal, should your job requires you to.

Prepare yourself to fail

It's the harsh truth of life that errors occur. If you're disappointed by the rejection of your job application initially Do not let it get you down enough to give up. Continue to try; nobody ever is unemployed He's just not found the perfect job to date. There are different skills for people, and no one is suitable to work in every industry on the planet. Continue to search until you find the job that helps you get through the day, but also feeds your hunger for work.

## Chapter 8: The Resume

Nearly every job you're applying for requires a resume, which is also known as the "CV," or "Curriculum Vitae." The document outlines your contact information, your previous job experience, abilities or volunteer projects, as well as your interests. Although most people see an resume as just an outline of information about your life, and that's correct, there are other ways to structure your resume in order to create the greatest impact on a prospective employer.

When creating your resume, take note of your previous work experiences. What were the jobs you've held? What qualifications did you gain? What are you looking to ensure that the person who views your application know about you?

It's okay even if you don't have any prior work experience. If you're just beginning your job search There are other items you could include in your application. Did you offer any kind of favors to your neighbors or family members? Do you have everyday chores or tasks you excel at?

Make sure to think this manner so there is something in your CV. If you are unable to think of enough details to fill a page, or the position that you're applying to doesn't require an application, it's always a good idea to have one on hand in case of need.

2 Strategies to Write a Successful Resume

In your list of previous experiences Be sure to mention details about the organization or organization where you worked, the job title or position you held and three bullet points that include phrases or sentences that describe your work and achievements. It's crucial to include words and action verbs throughout this part. Take a look at the examples below:

while working alongside my colleagues as a coworker, I had to wash dishes with my coworkers.

I was a dishwasher and aiding my coworkers in cleaning dishes

"Worked" can be described as an action verb. This second point describes your job tasks and helps you appear more productive.

Here are some more examples of terms to begin your descriptions using:

directed, organized, and oversaw the process, conceived, supervised created, guided, assisted with, devised it happen, made

These words show that you were active within your job, and explain how you have contributed and made a difference to your employer.

Another important aspect of making a great resume is providing quantitative measures of the performance. It is important to note that when you write your descriptions following the use of the action word, it is important to give a specific or fact-based measurement of the value you have added in your role as an employer.

Here's a different example:

Was a dishwasher in the workplace, helping my coworkers , and making sure they had clean dishes after doing my best during my shift

As a dishwasher, I was helping my coworkers develop the dishwashing process which increased the amount of dishes that are clean for them by 30 percent in just two weeks after beginning the job.

The second one shows that you can be a hard worker and be efficient, and you are committed to improving the efficiency of the company you work for.

The way you arrange your resume is largely your choice. But there are certain things that you must include in your resume.

1. Contact Information - ensure that you include your complete name and email address, as well as your telephone

number, as well as the town or city in which you reside on your resume's top. This way, anyone looking at your resume will know who to reach you.

2. Education - write down your education record. If you've only been to high school, write the school name next to your name. If you've attended colleges, universities or any other type of postsecondary education, list them on your resume. However, don't list the high school you attended.

3. Work Experience This is an important element in your resume. List your most recent work first and if you're out of space, pick the most important or challenging positions you've held or jobs you're proud of.

4.Leadership/Volunteering/Extracurricular/Other - you can also include a section that includes types of work where you were not paid, or areas of your life that you are accomplished in but are not part of your career.

5. Skills or interests - This section could be located at the bottom of your resume, should there be space over. You can include your hobbies and interests outside of work , allowing the prospective employer to get an idea of your personality and passions.

It is important to ensure that your resume is of one page. You do not want to force someone to go through a lengthy unorganized document, and you don't have to list every single thing you've done throughout your life on a resume. Only include what you believe is most important and will make you appear nice!

In the following page, you will see an image of an example resume. Take note of the way it's organized. The spacing and font have been adjusted to accommodate the maximum amount of information possible on one page. Additionally, it's well organized and precise. The job descriptions include action verbs, as well as fact-based measurements of the performance.

Your resume doesn't need to appear identical however, as you grow and acquire more work experiences, your resume should appear like this.

## Chapter 9: Interview Questions and Answer

You've already received suggestions on how to prepare for an interview, and also what you should do in the course of your interview. Now, you might be thinking what you should do or what to prepare for questions that might be being asked from you?

The majority of the types of questions your interviewer is likely to ask the interviewer are merely elaborations of the information you have on your CV. Keep in mind that interviews place you under pressure and could lead you to overlook important information, so review your resume. If it's the focal point of the discussion it will be easier to share your knowledge as well as your accomplishments and qualifications. Be sure to plan and reflect on what you've accomplished or contributed to your previous organisations that can't be documented in your CV.

If you've done your research on the company, its industry, and the interviewer, it will be simple to answer basic questions such as "What is your knowledge about the company?" Because these facts can find on the website of the company or in blogs online. There's no reason to you to attend your interview unprepared because it's easy to find these information on the internet.

PARADE Method

This is a method of responding to questions about resumes for job interviews You can utilize it to write concise and effective responses to frequently asked resume-related questions. It can also remind you to find all the essential details needed to respond to these questions.

The acronym PARADE which is a reference to:

P Roblem

A Participated consequence

R ole

A action

The Decision-Making Rationale

E nd-Result

1.) PROBLEM - What is the issue that you or your team confronted

2.) ANTICIPATED CONSEQUENCE - What impact did your company or you have to face if the issue remained without resolution?

3.) Role How did you play your part in solving this issue?

4) Action What action did you do? What was your response?

5) DESCRIPTION-MAKING RATIONALE - Describe the reason you chose to take the decision you took. What other alternatives were you considering? Why did you decide not to choose other alternatives?

6) Final Results -- When you completed the task you did, what transpired? What was the result?

Here are a few examples of the most challenging questions you could be asked during your interview, along with the best ways you can tackle these questions confidently. There's no single method to answer these questions. The way you answer these questions depends on your personal situation your job interview and position you're applying for and your experience So what you'll find below are suggestions for how to tackle the question, and draw on your skills and experience to provide an answer that will demonstrate to the interviewer why you're the perfect candidate for the job.

1.) Why do you not tell me about you?

You may think this is an opportunity to you to share with the interviewer about your life. But it's not. It's actually an opportunity to inform the interviewer of your skills and experience, and why they make you an ideal candidate for the job you're applying for. What you can do is to highlight your strengths in your education, experience, and qualifications that are tailored to your job's description. But, if the interviewer is actually asking you questions about your family history or education , don't hesitate to mention your experiences and qualifications. However, keep it short and in the scope of your interview. Be careful not to get personal and don't share too much.

2.) What are the reasons I should work with you?

Similar to the question above, this is an opportunity to discuss your personal experiences and skills which make you ideal for the job they're trying to fill. This is the perfect opportunity to make yourself stand out from the other candidates. You , along with other applicants were chosen because of specific qualifications which the company believed would be suitable for the job However, now is the opportunity to convince your interviewers that you're most suitable to be hired.

3.) What is your weak point?

The way people tackle this issue isn't exactly accurate. They look for a strength, then create it into an area of weakness, when it's not. For instance, telling an interviewer that your weak point is in being a perfectionist isn't a sign of weakness. Tell them the truth. Let them know a weakness in your character or your personality and then explain what you're doing to overcome or correcting this weakness. It's also a good way for interviewers to know how attentive and critical you are of yourself as well as your flaws.

4) What would your clients/supervisor/workmates say about you?

It is actually an assessment of how you're doing at keeping your professional relationships. In addition, this is an opportunity to review your references. If you're able, you should take the time to obtain letters of recommendation to present to the interviewer. Let them speak for you. However, try to be honest and put your shoes on those people and reflect on how you've been as a client/subordinate/workmate to them.

5) Did you experience an instance where you questioned the status of the game?

This one can be somewhat difficult to answer, because it asks you to explain how you challenged processes as well as the way things are done within your previous organization. What you can do to answer this particular question is to explain to the interviewer the procedure or process that you disrupted, the reason you decided to interrupt it, and then explain what benefits was derived from the disruption. This shows you're willing and able to test different things to enhance the efficiency of your company This is always an excellent thing to think about.

6) What do you think of your self in the next five years?

This question is a demonstration of you are aware of your professional choice as well as your profession of choice. This is also a chance to demonstrate to interviewers the goals you have set for yourself and your company, and how you will meet these goals. It is possible to draw upon your experience and skills here and demonstrate to the interviewer that you have set objectives and who will work hard to meet these targets. Determination and ambition are beneficial traits for every employee.

7.) Have you had disputes with your colleagues or with your boss? What was your solution to the conflict?

Interviewers will ask this question because keeping a good civil relation with your coworkers or supervisors is essential for any workplace that is conducive to work. This also shows how you're managing conflict within the immediate environment of your work. This will also show how you keep your professional relationships and the way you work with people who are not your ideals.

If you've not been involved in an event like that at work be truthful and inform the interviewer this. There's no reason to be making up stories about things that didn't take place. If, however, you were a victim of it, make sure you inform your interviewer about how you dealt with the conflict and the way you resolved the problem with the individuals who were involved.

8.) Why did you decide to leave/why did you decide to leave your current employer?

This is important as it's an opportunity for your present employers to determine whether you're able to criticize your former or current employer. However they'll also are looking to find out what the former company was unable to provide or give you which led you to quit them. The best option is to avoid praising the company you left and then talk your potential to grow and be a valuable asset to the new business. Interviewers appreciate a candidate who is eager to learn and is eager to improve while also is aware of the skills set and knows what skills he/she can contribute to the team.

9) What are your motivators?

There are occasions when it's easy to want to quit or like to quit the project. Sometimes, the work is difficult and you aren't sure how to overcome it, and your interviewers know this. Asking about what drives you is a way to gauge how easy it is to give up the determination you have to complete an assignment. Being able to identify your motivations also shows your self-awareness, since you know the factors that keep you motivated.

The purpose of this question is to provide interviewers with understanding of what motivates you, what prevents you from doing your best the job, what values you place first and what you like doing. Be aware that this question doesn't focus on the reasons that drive you to take on the job, so stop discussing the credit card debts you have or the cost of the wedding you're planning!

10) What is it that sets you apart from the other candidates?

Another exercise in self-awareness. This is your chance to show the interviewer what you're willing to bring to the business that your competition do not. Also it shows how prepared and ready you are to be for the job and also a method to determine if you do have the skills to be hired.

Make sure to be sure to keep it to your CV. include your experience along with your work experience, as well as your skills. Concentrate on the value you'll be for the company. Your accomplishments and skills sets that relate to the position. Be sure to connect it to the description of the job being offered. You should be so attractive and it would be foolish to let them pass on you!

If you have other questions, simply be honest , but not too negative to your potential employers. For instance, if you've been fired, you can claim that your "parted with the boss." The principle is to always justify your claim with a previous experience or a certification you've earned.

Do not lie during your interview as it could end up being disastrous for you, particularly in the event that an employer you've applied to is able to find out. Remember that the person you interview wants to get to know your personality and assessing whether you're a good fit for the position and in the workplace. What you must demonstrate to them by your character the qualifications you have, as well as your work experience.

# Chapter 10: Examples of Professional Themes

Examples of themes for professional use include:

1. The entrepreneur who is drawn to working with young startups and other businesses may opt for the idea of innovation. This implies that they are inclined to think out of the box and prefer to work in an inefficient, slow-moving company, where lots of things need to be done and decisions must be taken before changes can be implemented.

2. The person who is a workhorse who is driven by getting things accomplished may opt for the topic of personal growth and efficiency. If this is the case you could be driven by the desire to maintain your personal growth and improvement. The majority of them do not require external motivation or structure since they are self-sufficient and have the ability to meet their own standards.

3. If you are a fan of working with nonprofits and similar organizations, then perhaps your focus is the Philanthropist. This theme is motivated by the desire to aid others, be it business, individuals or a mixture of both.

4. While not many people would admit it, there are some who are motivated by money. This isn't bad if you are able to recognize your real desire. When you embrace it, you will be able to have financial security as your main objective and show that, by your determination to constantly increase your financial status and you've made a lot of progress in your professional life.

5. If you are always looking for the opportunity to assist in managing the work of others or to supervise them, maybe your career is based on a leadership concept. This topic will assist you to answer interview questions about how you are able to motivate and

communicate with other people to achieve specific goals in your business.

Whatever the subject matter be sure you are able to clearly define it in a couple of words. If it's unclear or not easy to communicate, revisit it and work on it until it's an easy thing to comprehend.

This will allow you to determine the flow of your responses It's essential to identify your style in a clear manner, then clearly explain it, and be aware that it will be evident in the majority of your answers to your interview.

The next section will be able to see the answers and details related to some of the most frequently asked interview questions. It is recommended to pick your theme prior to studying the answers. However, you should go back to your theme at the close to determine whether it's still relevant to you.

Sometimes, rereading the answers and questions will assist you in finding an authentic or more lively subject matter that you can employ as the narrative basis of your interview questions.

# Chapter 11: What's holding Your Interview Success Back? Reviewing which thoughts do the damage

"What was I thinking that has led me to create my life as this is?" - Phil Laut Best-Selling Author of Self-Help

Even with your goals set and motivation formulated and high however, you may find that something's blocking your progress. The negative beliefs you hold regarding yourself and your abilities as an interviewee or job candidate could be a major hurdle.

It doesn't matter if you're trying to be more confident and appear more confident, you must remember what you can say or how to blow them away by presenting your work knowledge. If you're struggling with doubts about yourself as a candidate , or perhaps an attitude that seems to be focused on what you believe to be your flaws it is important to work on this. You might not believe that you're a victim of any beliefs that could be holding you back , but be careful as they could be lurking in your unconscious. It's funny that they don't have to be truthful (and usually they aren't) to to block your path and hinder you from reaching your full potential.

Although there may be some truth in them , the positive is that when you spend some time in identifying these negative or restricting views, you can turn the tables completely and apply the information to gain.

This is actually quite easy to achieve, however you have to be truthful about yourself. No one else should be aware of your thoughts that are negative, however you need to take a deep dive and confront them with a straight face. Then, we'll use them to assist you in reaching your desired goals.

Keep this thought in mind: when you arrive to talk with them, the interviewer is likely to be looking for the solution to their issues. All you need to do is to convince yourself, and then the interviewer to believe that it is true!

* Dissecting What You Believe

You'll need something to write about in this case. This is an extremely important stage because we'll apply what you're about discover later on - therefore, don't try to skim this step.

Let me first affirm that there's no reason to feel uneasy or foolish in analyzing your own thought process. The majority of us aren't accustomed to questioning what we believe in , especially those "beliefs" are a part of our own. But this is the way most successful people advance.

If you're not sure that you're able to come in a professional manner or present yourself in a professional manner when you are in the interview process to secure your dream job, those are your negative thoughts at work. Even if it seems like that you don't have any negative thoughts about yourself, check out the following questions.

Answer as completely and honestly as you are able to. Make sure to write the answers in a notebook and store them secure as we'll need them in the future.

What's stopping you from being the ideal candidate for interviewing to be hired?

or

What's stopping you from getting the job you really want?

Take the time to truly question yourself. Here are some typical responses that people have when doing this type of self-questioning on their work.

"They'll believe I'm old."

"I might not be skilled enough."

"They believe I'm way too old."

"Other candidates may have more experience than I do."

"I find myself anxious during interviews."

"There's too many competitors for the type of job I'd like to have."

Your answers could differ, however you need to engage in this. Be as damning as you like. You're searching for the thoughts that hold your back, so if you're not honest with yourself here, it won't help.

Maybe your memory isn't as strong in giving the answers you plan to typical interview questions? Maybe you feel anxious or anxious when before an interviewer or panel? Maybe you're not sure if your technical capabilities are as impressive as other prospective candidates' will be?

I have heard of a frustrated job seeker who believed that the main issue she had was that she never seemed to be well-dressed for interviews, no matter what was wearing! No matter what you believe that you think, all you need to do now is to uncover your negative beliefs about yourself and the ability of you to stand out at an interview and note them down.

Perhaps you believe that you'll never be more professional in interviews, or that you'll get to a certain point in your career, and that any significant advances will require many hours and efforts.

Many older adults who have lost work say that they feel like "impossible" as they begin to think about getting back into work later in their lives. They often think to themselves "Who are you fooling?" whenever they think of applying for jobs or even obtaining the same position once more.

Their list could include like the one above: "I'm too old to be able to find an acceptable job once more."

Another negative obstacle common to all is the refusal to give up due to beliefs such as:

"I'd nie be quite as great than the others."

Give this a lot of thought and then try to make an idea of at least 10 ideas.

This list is the main reason for your current position and also for the reasons you're not secure enough or attain the results you desire in your interviews.

In the next few days, we'll transform this negativity into something truly productive and positive.

## Chapter 12: "Describe Yourself In One Word."

Our lives are complex and multifaceted human beings, and the use of a single word to describe us may be untrue. It's tempting to choose broad goals like "unique" as well as an overall, secure option like "industrious." But the answers you choose to give are generally generic and insufficient for employers to understand. Instead, consider the particular gap you're trying for (or the job you're seeking) and then tailor your answer to match.

Select a phrase that is compatible with your values and also who your company is or what kind of candidate they'd like to recruit. If, for instance, the company is innovating then you will prefer to stick with "classical" as a term. It is also possible to choose one of your personal traits that will not alter regardless of the situation. A characteristic like "resilient" can be considered more suitable because it shows that you're the type of person to be able to complete your tasks and could also show that you are an ideal fit with the culture. Whatever your character trait try to tie it to your company or the job. Let me give you an additional example:

If you're looking for a job in housekeeping and you are applying for a housekeeping position, you could use words like attentive, diligent efficient, or attentive. These are the qualities which will surely help you when you are in a position in which the employer expects its employees to follow strict guidelines for tasks such as guest service at hotels and cleaning, as well as efficient management of time they devote to various tasks throughout the day.

"What is your greatest strength?"

Interviewers ask the question in order to find out the strengths that align with requirements of the business and the duties of the position. The interviewer would like to know whether you're a suitable candidate for the position for which you're being interviewed.

Your answer will help the employer determine if you're the best candidate for the job or not. This is for instance, that if the position you're seeking involves accounting, it's not the best choice to emphasize your skills in planning events.

It is important to demonstrate that you possess the characteristics that the interviewer is looking for in the ideal candidate. We possess an array of variety of qualities that employers are looking for in candidates they hire, however certain of them are specific to the job and company. So, the best way to answer the question is to describe your experience and abilities have that directly relate to the job you're applying for.

To protect yourself, make a list of your qualifications in the job advertisement. job, and then write down your abilities that are in line with the qualifications needed. This list could comprise education or training as well as soft skills, or even your previous job experience. Then, narrow the list to three to five strengths. Then, you should have an example next for each skill that shows how you've used this specific strength at some point in your life.

By doing this, you'll be able to discuss specific strengths when an interviewer inquires about that of you. If you answer to the question, you'll be demonstrating an attribute that matches the skills required by the company.

Let's take a look at an illustration.

A great strength to be mentioned is your work ethic "I have a solid dedication to work." If you are asked to describe your reasoning, you state, "when working on any task, I do not always look to meet deadlines. Instead I prefer to finish the tasks ahead of time. In the last three months, I was awarded an enormous bonus for completing my most recent three reports 7 days earlier than the deadline."

*"Tell me About Yourself."*

This isn't simply a throwaway question to many interviewers. Managers who interview candidates typically pose the question open-ended in the hope to gain insights from you on what you think makes you an ideal candidate to the position. It is also used to find out about the candidate's priorities. This question gives them a clear idea of who you are.

Sometimes, interviewers will inquire about the level of confidence and clarity, as they wish to determine how they'd show themselves to customers, clients and coworkers if they are hired.

Let's get started by defining what you shouldn't do.

Don't discuss anything personal, such as your family, hobbies or children. Don't talk about your personal story, or consider sharing some of the details of the challenges you are confronted with at work--perhaps as many do and suggest that you were a candidate for this job because your commute was awful or your employer was rude and the like.

Absolutely, you shouldn't make a list of your resume and go in detail your education and work experience. In addition to sounding excessively long and unfocused, these responses can send interviewers red flags, indicating that you're just trying to get out of a negative situation at work and that you're not committed to the job. If you choose to take the second option you'll be losing a great chance. The interviewers should will have read your CV prior to inviting for an interview. it is not necessary to go over it.

What are you going to do to answer to this question?

Be sure to explain clear and concisely - how you meet the requirements to be considered for the position and the reason you're interested in the position.

Before you start putting together your selling points, you should take your time to go through the job description that is included in the advertisement advertising the position, and also study the company. You must know what employers are looking for in terms knowledge and experience.

Then, write an outline of your strengths, abilities and experience that make you uniquely qualified for the job, followed by the main reasons why you're seeking the position. Focus on your motivations for pursuing your career, such as the desire to increase your skills and gain greater responsibilities. End with a concise paragraph that explains why the company appeals to you. Let's look at an example of a reply in response to the following question: "tell me about yourself."

"For the last four years, I've been employed in the capacity of an assistant to administrative. The department that handles accounts is an up-and-coming startup which is where I am currently working. I am responsible for meeting, travel scheduling, and meeting planning for 20 staff members and five executive. Additionally, I write reports, presentations and correspondence.

My colleagues recognize me for being a neat and meticulous team player. I'm a very good communication expert and never fail to meet deadlines. I also can take on more than one job at the same time. In my reviews of performance my supervisor will always say that she appreciates my dedication and professionalism.

With this level of experience I'm looking for a chance to take the next step in my professional career. I would like to work within an organization such as this one, which is driven by innovation, something I've been a keenly interested in for quite a while."

"Where Are You Going to Be in X Years?"

This is a question that interviewers will use to determine if your career objectives are in line with the objectives of the business. It can also help them determine whether you're likely to be working for their company for a long time, or whether you'll only be working for a short period of time.

I understand that questions about the future are difficult to answer, especially during an interview However, you must provide a truthful answer but make sure you remain pertinent to the field and the job. For example, if are looking for a finance job it is not appropriate to say that your aim is to start your own fitness and yoga center.

In order to be adequately prepared to answer this question, you must look into a suitable career path that flows from the job you are applying for. The main question you're trying to answer at this moment is "how how long will an typical worker be working in the position?" In addition, "what are the next steps in the span of one year?"

Certain companies provide clear pathways in their careers section. However, in order to get the most accurate view you might need consult with experts around you in your field, like alumni, friends professional associations, your family.

If, for instance, you are a certified lab technician and you are looking for a technician position at a specific hospital and you'd like to advance into management then you must look into the institution to determine the likelihood of lab technicians working in technician management positions.

Start by looking for open laboratory technician positions on the careers section of the website, so that you can ensure that the business is hiring. You can then look up LinkedIn pages of laboratory technician supervisors working in the hospital. If this is a potential career option, you'll be able see the people who have made that decision.

Let's look at an alternative answer to the question "where do you envision yourself in four years' time?"

"I want to keep developing my technical knowledge as part of this group. I've also observed that there are a lot of laboratory technician managers at Woodley Hospital move from staff lab technician to technician manager. That is something that I am interested in to be a part of my career path over four years."

## Chapter 13: The Interview Behaviour

Many people are unsure of what to do in an interview. Interviews can be stressful and cause bad behavior for people. However, there are ways to ensure you're acting appropriately in the course of an interview. A lot of your interview depends on how you conduct yourself. It's not only about how you talk. Your character can play a significant role in determining whether you are offered an interview or are not. There are a few things you should keep an eye on when interviewing.

Two bad things to avoid are to chew mints or gum and using the word slang in your speech. It's not attractive and you can't hide it and is offensive. Don't put anything inside your mouth in an interview. Make sure you speak well and clearly. You don't want to appear immature or unprofessional.

There are some things to be aware of that could make a massive impact on your impression of the interviewer.

Confidence

You need to go to an interview with confidence. Nobody would like to observe someone who is clearly not convinced that they are able to perform the task. It's an important balance since you don't wish to appear too confident. You must be confident of yourself, yet not overly confident about it. The person interviewing you must know that you're competent to do the job but also be able to get along with your colleagues.

Achievements must be true. They should be stated in a straightforward manner without excessive amount of details. The interviewer must be aware of the nature of these individuals however, you don't have to boast about them.

Attitude

Positive emotions are more attractive over negative attitudes. It is important to smile and appear to be a cheerful person to speak to. Be aware that you're trying to make yourself appear attractive before the person you interview. Avoid looking in the face and expressing disapproval if you are told something that's different from what you desired. Make sure you wait for the right moment to talk about your the issue.

Eye Contact

You must maintain an eye-to-eye contact with anyone you're speaking to, or else you look unconfident or unprofessional. You don't want to look like you're bored since this person is making the decision on whether you'll be offered the job. You wouldn't want to be able to tolerate the way you behave from another person, therefore, don't glance at the other people in the room.

Body Language

The body language of your body can speak volumes but it's not coming out from your mouth. It is important to sit straight and remain aware. There are some essential things to be aware of when you sit through an interview.

The first rule is to not play around when someone else is speaking. It can distract and make people think you're not secure or paying attention. When it comes to distractions hand gestures can be distracting too, so be careful to avoid using them for too long.

In the event that you bite your lips between questions or squint your eyes, you'll appear to be not truthful or trying to conjure up an answer.

When you sit down with hands crossed you're looking like you are a little aloof and inaccessible. Make sure your arms are relaxed and on your lap.

Gestures should not be used as a substitute for speaking. Spend some time thinking of a solution rather than shrugging your shoulders when aren't sure of a solution. It makes you appear as if you're trying to come up with an answer. Head shakes and nods are also not suitable in situations where you are asked questions.

The final thing you want to stay clear of is crying. It is a sign of boredom, therefore make sure that you are healthy and well-rested to prevent yawning.

*First Impressions*

Your first impression is likely be a positive one for the interviewer, and leave the most impression. It is important for this impression to be the best you can give. There are a few ways to help make this process easier.

*The Do's and Don'ts of First Impressions*

These are the points to be aware of as you begin your interview.

Make sure you are polite. People in the reception and lobby areas are watching you and giving feedback, so ensure that you're polite to anyone you come across.

While waiting, you should sit down and act as if you were being interviewing. You could be being observed for your behavior in the absence of anyone else.

Give a firm handshake and smile when greeting interviewers.

You must stand till the person interviewing you has instructed you to sit down out of respect.

Make sure you are prepared for your interview.

Dress in line with the position you're applying for.

Make sure you arrive on time or earlier to demonstrate that you are punctual.

You can use the name of the person interviewing you.

Keep your eyes open throughout the day.

Make comments light and positive.

Make sure you speak clearly and with clarity in the interview.

Other than refreshments offered to the person interviewing.

The Do's and Don'ts of First Impressions

There are many habits we all share that shouldn't be revealed in an interview.

Avoid eating or drinking as you wait for your interview.

Don't bring out your phone at any time during or in the time of interview. It can make you appear distracted.

Don't be aggressive or insistent.

Don't focus on the money. Let the interviewer talk about it first.

Don't be uninterested in the job or company.

Do not be defensive in your questions.

Don't make a fuss about former employers or co-workers.

Do not respond simply with no or yes answers.

Don't make excuses for poor points in work history.

Don't excuse yourself from having to go to the bathroom.

Do not ask for refreshments.

These factors can help to make the interview successful and make the first impressions made by you to be positive ones that stay on with your interviewer.

# Chapter 14: Different types of Interviews

Interviews for business are different from the ones you've had at this point. They're generally more lengthy, multi-step processes. The most effective example you be able to find is an interview you completed to gain admission into graduate school. In this section, we'll examine different styles of interviewing to provide you with an idea of what you could be facing and also the specific types of interviews you might encounter. All the information we've provided previously is still applicable to these kinds of interviews, however, each has specific aspects to consider. These suggestions will make sure that you don't get surprised by a manner of interviewing that you've never experienced before.

Traditional vs Behavioral

There's been a shift in recent times between traditional interviews and an approach known as "behavioral" interviews. In traditional interviews, the questions are usually more hypothetical "If you were required to connect two branches How would you ensure that the process was smooth?" Behavioral interview questions however tend to focus on the actual experiences the candidate has. While this can be more efficient in determining the ability however, it isn't always easy to answer questions when you're fresh from school with no working knowledge. The key to finding an give a truthful answer and still provides your interviewer with something to work from is to know what the are really trying to find out. Instead of answering the question based on its the face value, consider the question being asked to learn about your personality, skills and talents. For instance, if the interviewer asks "How did you manage to blend different departments or branches?" you may feel confused. If you've not had the experience, you might be hesitant to answer. But what the examiner is trying to determine is whether you are able to bring together different groups of individuals. This is a broad range of skills , such as making plans for difficult situations and settling disputes among employees. It is also important to determine if you have the character to unite people through compassion, kindness and awe. Do you have an instance where you've displayed these qualities and skills? Think of the questions this manner, with regard of the questions they're asking below the surface, will help you answer any question they may throw at you. Here are some questions interviewers have switched to after the introduction of behavioral interviewing into style. When you look through this list, consider what the interviewer wants to find out with each and the ways you could show your expertise in these areas.

\* What was your least-favorite part of your previous job? What was the thing that most frustrated you?

\* Can you provide me with an any instance where you've needed to take a risk to complete the task?

Please give me an example of an initiative that you were very happy for you to complete.

\* What is it that means for your success?

\* How do you determine whether to send an email to an employee or speak in person? Could you provide some examples of messages that you could convey through both channels?

Please tell me about a time when you helped ease tensions between two people working for or with you.

\* How did you exceed your expectations in work? What was that expectation from you?

\* If you are faced with an assignment which is time-sensitive how can you make sure that deadlines are adhered to? Please share a moment when this method worked for you.

* What kind of leadership styles make work most satisfying for you? What characteristics of an employer make it hard for you to be a fan of?

Please tell me the story of the worst moment you've experienced at work. How did you deal with the stress?

How do you decide which tasks to delegate? Provide an instance of how your strategy for delegation has been successful in solving a problem at work.

• How will you deal with the criticism you receive at work? Let me know about the time you received negative feedback , and the way you handled it.

Try to frame your responses to these questions to reflect on what your individual capabilities will benefit the goals of your company. Even if you've not experienced the same situations it's possible to see the things they're trying to learn about you. We'll go over the first couple of concerns to assist you in getting feel of the process.

* The first question asks how you manage tension and conflict. Every job is filled with the possibility of some unpleasantness and the person interviewing you must be confident that you can handle it without negatively impacting your performance or making you angry. Discuss difficult times and how you remained in your cool throughout the process.

* This question may appear to be a way to determine the risk-taker, but when you look more deeply, you will discover that the issue is actually about planning. When an opportunity to make a leap has to be made, the steps taken prior to and after are as crucial in the same way as taking the chance itself. Make sure that your interviewer knows that you're aware of this by providing showing how to lay the foundations for a planned carefully thought-out step.

* This isn't simply a way to show off. It's a chance that the person interviewing you can discover the strengths you have, without having to ask you directly. People generally have the greatest satisfaction with jobs they excel in This is an opportunity for them to determine what your actual strengths are, not only what you think you have.

You can tell that many questions come with a couple of "levels." In the event that you aren't able to solution to the top of what the question appears to ask, consider further.

Interviews via phone

Interviews via phone are typically used to conduct "screening interview" or to ensure that hiring is taking place over long distances. Screening interviews can be thought of similar to interviews that are pre-arranged. They tend to be quick, lasting anywhere between 20 or even an hour. The aim that the HR employee who conducts the interview is will be to identify the top candidates to forward for the interviewer to conduct the more thorough, in-depth interview in the future. After you've done your research and prepared, you're likely overflowing with enthusiasm to demonstrate how competent and eager to go. The interview probably isn't going to offer you with the chance to talk about your well-crafted stories about your professional experience, but. The screening process is designed to determine if your expectations for salary as well as your career goals and expertise are appropriate to the job. It doesn't mean you should just list the information, however. The HR representative at the other end the line will be watching closely the way you communicate your thoughts across, how friendly you are, and if the interview goes smoothly.

One thing you should be aware prior to stepping into an interview you resume, is that this is probably the sole information they have on your current situation and the interview may be based on that. The interviewer is likely to go through your work timeline, step-by-step in asking you to elaborate on your job, the skills that you needed, as well as the reasons why you quit every job. If you have gaps in your education or employment background, you must be able to discuss the gaps in a manner that doesn't sound unfocused or sloppy. Another side of that side is that you should not be apprehensive about your lifestyle choices regardless of whether they make your resume look fragmented. The hiring staff is educated to know the many factors and causes that impact our career paths So don't count yourself out just because you're worried about how your resume appears. Define the circumstances which led to the inconsistencies with a straightforward one or two-sentence answer. "I faced a family emergency that demanded my full focus. The situation is resolved now however, and I'm prepared to give my best in this situation" is all you need.

Try to ensure that the discussion is going quickly. If the interviewer is asking about a particular job or particular detail, offer some sentences that are pertinent, before asking if it covers what they were seeking. This will ensure that you don't spend the entire time allotted to you by one answer and giving a distorted description of your knowledge.

Prepare for your meeting by finding an place that has good reception, silent and free of distractions. Dress comfortably and keep an empty glass of water on hand in case your throat starts to get wet or scratchy.

To prepare yourself for the phone screen interview to prepare for your phone screen interview, ask your mock interviewer ask you a few questions regarding the job and your qualifications for the position. When they ask these questions make sure to spice up the interview with your personal style to convey a positive impression without taking all of an interviewer's attention.

If the interview via phone will replace an in-person interview due distance or another reason, the procedure remains exact the same. The research and mock interviews and the more advanced skills in conversationcan all be used to this situation. It is possible to not need to wear the dress code.

Video Interviews

Video interviews are becoming more widespread. Originally, they were used to hire people from afar but now they are being used for interviews in towns because they're easier for a variety of scenarios. For instance, if lots of individuals need to be present to interview them an interview via video can help, regardless of the distance.

In the majority of cases preparation for this interview is like preparing for an interview in person. It is important to dress appropriately for the event (even pants! There's no telling the time you'll need to stand up for a reason.) Unless it's stated that it is a screening and you're expected to give all the time you can on this particular interview that you do for any other.

There are some specific guidelines for this type of interview. It is common for interviewers to request to "share the screen" in the course of an interview. This allows them to view the screen you're using and redirect your computer to various websites or resources that could assist in your interview. Check that your Internet browsing is not the sole one open, your desktop has been clear and you've cleared the history of your browser to minimize the chance that a wrong click could lead you to the wrong website. Employers have heard nightmare stories of having chat windows that are open, with unsuitable conversations, or tabs that are open to request "help with an interview.

Be sure when they do view the screen you've done your best enough to provide an enjoyable experience. This is a great way in purchasing goodwill.

Check to see that your laptop is running at full capacity and that you're located in an area that's peaceful and that you are connected to the internet properly. The slightest glitch or disconnect could not hurt you specifically in your interview but they can disrupt your flow and cause you to be nervous.

Finally, ensure that you don't let the disconnect of screen-to screen communication does not fool in a sense of sense of casualness. This type of interview has the same formality and weight that an in-person interview could.

Breakfast or dinner Interviews

Interviews in restaurants could add another level of stress which you might not have considered. This isn't necessarily the best scenario however, it could occur.

If it happens, you'll be content to have a plan for these scenarios.

A majority of the time, the hiring manager will suggest the restaurant. However, there's a possibility that you'll be asked to select an area that is convenient. If this happens, select one that's easy for the interviewer to reach. Restaurants should have moderately priced and hopefully , it will have delicious food. If you're able to pick a place you've previously been to and loved then you're in luck. Reserve the most peaceful table that there is.

It's much more likely you'll arrive at the restaurant you've been invited to, in time and having looked at the menu on the internet. In reality, you need to conduct a lot of research regarding the restaurant. Examine the traffic and parking issues so that you are able that you have enough time. If you are sensitive to food ensure that you be accommodated there. If not consume food before leaving and choose the most simple thing to nibble on.

Beyond that the rules are identical to a first date but without alcohol. Choose a dish that is simple to eat, not dirty, and easy to eat. There's lots of conversations. Concerning the alcohol it's possible to hear you can have one or two glasses, but it's best to stay clear of.

Group Interviews

Similar to video interviews and group interviews, group interviews are getting more common every day. Particularly in highly competitive markets hiring managers may consider a group interview to be necessary to sort through a large number of applicants quickly. Although it's a great idea to them, the process could make your experience more challenging. The pace and style of conversation you're used to are absent, and replaced by a more complex and intricate group dynamics.

In order to make this process work for you, and not for you, then you'll have to be able to take part in a discussion group or some other type of activity. In the early years this was known as "playing effectively with other children," and that's something you must do when you apply for jobs. Interviewers are seeking candidates who are able to collaborate as an organization. One who isn't able to speak loudly or constantly interrupts will not give the sense of cooperation you're hoping to create. Keep in mind that effective leadership means not pushing another person around and at times, giving someone else the responsibility of running an initiative. It's not easy to discern the difference between humility and confidence however, you must ensure that the interviewers are to be sure that you know the entire range of the management demands.

Third, Second and More

Following a screening interview you might be asked for another, more thorough interview. The second interview can be scheduled following a first formal interview. It is common to be informed beforehand how many interviews will be held during the process, however this isn't always the case. Interviews with groups are typically held during the later rounds of interviews If you're planning to go back to the interview, you should be aware that it's possible.

It's likely that you'll need to respond to a number of the same questions every round. Keep your energy up. The feeling of fatigue is normal however, you'll have to combat it and continue to be your most professional and most energetic self.

## Chapter 15: Why Should We Hire You?

What are they looking to learn?

Do you feel confident in the skills you have will be useful in this position?

Let's admit it. If you're not sure of your capabilities and abilities, you might not be as good as you think.

The incorrect answer

I'm going to work for hours.

This isn't the correct answer. In most cases people will give this answer. that people offer. It's not necessarily in these words but frequently they have the same meaning.

If you answer this question, they will tell them, we're expecting you to be a hard worker. Everyone is required to be a hard worker.

If you're offering this as a solution you're simply repeating the obvious. Keep in mind why the person is asking. They want to know whether you're confident in your capabilities. If you're confident in your abilities that you are confident, they will be.

The best answer

My expertise and skills will surpass the expectations set by this position.

This is a sure answer. They are trying to gauge confidence in you here because that's the test they're looking for. You must be confident in your capabilities and capabilities.

It's always beneficial to elaborate a bit on your response. You can do this by listing the outcomes you've achieved due to your skills and knowledge. This will bring it to life. They will be able to see how your talents and skills are a perfect match.

Do you remember a moment when you were unsuccessful?

What are they looking to learn?

The mistakes you've made and the lessons you have learned from the mistakes you made and how you can avoid them.

Nobody is perfect. What they are looking for is that you're eager be willing to make mistakes in order to make improvements. They want to see an individual who is constantly trying and eager to learn. Someone who can accept criticism and benefit of constructive feedback.

The incorrect answer

I'm not able to think of an occasion.

This is nothing more than an excuse to cover up. Many people believe that by admitting mistakes , they are hurting their chances. But the reverse is the case.

When you claim that you don't come up with anything they'll assume that you are not paying attention or oblivious to your errors. Remember, everyone makes mistakes. This is the way we learn. The question is asked to determine if you have learned and want to grow.

The correct answer

Discuss the circumstances and explain what you did. In depth describe the circumstances as well as the steps you took and the result. Make sure to mention the lessons you've learned and how you could improve. Explain what you learned next time around or you will do it again.

Here's an illustration...

My team didn't receive gratitude when they had achieved great results. I noticed that the sales figures were beginning to decline. Then I began thinking about ways to improve the situation.

I realized that perhaps I didn't provide them with enough credit for their achievements.

So I decided to make a point to congratulate each customer whenever I noticed something excellent. Within a short period of time the sales figures started to increase again. From that point on, I've been doing this for a long time, to make me a better supervisor. It's something I'll do forever.

This question reveals the error and the lessons you took from the mistake. You learned from the mistake.

The fact that you made this error does not harm your chances of being noticed.

Instead they will be able to see how you've grown more efficient.

We want to know about your most memorable achievement?

What are they looking to know?

What is most important to you? What are you passionate about the most? What is it that you enjoy doing? it?

They want to see more proof that you be a pleasure to complete the tasks they asked for.

The answer does not have to come from work. It could come from any thing that you face in your daily life.

The incorrect answer

Talking about something insignificant. Do not give something that's very small. The time it took to get your dog toilet-trained isn't a huge deal. Look for something more substantial.

If you provide a nebulous example, it's going to show that you don't put the importance of anything that is significant.

You'll appear to be an average performer. That's not what they are looking for.

The best answer

Everybody has done something. It's virtually impossible to live your life without accomplishing something.

Go through all of the years you've lived. Remember when you were a kid and then as an adolescent. Think back to the first time you worked. Find something. You'll surely discover it.

Let me take you. When I was 16 years old I would attend these dance parties. They were typically organised by people other than me. The last time I saw one was several months and I'd been not aware of it.

I inquired about how to organize an event hall. I inquired about how other people had successfully arranged refreshments and how they could invite guests.

I was able to do all the lessons I learned. Within less than two weeks I attended was a dance session. This is not bad for a normal sixteen-year-old.

It doesn't necessarily have to come an issue at work. In my case the incident was not related to work. It does demonstrate my ability to plan.

# Chapter 16: High Qualities Respected by Employers

Work ethic that is strong -

According to numerous studies the ability to work hard is among the top traits employers look at in applicants. People with a solid work ethics always have integrity. Integrity is about being honest and doing the right thing always regardless of whether anyone is paying attention. Integrity-minded employees have positive relationships with their colleagues who surround them, and these who trust them. the integrity of their employees. They also are disciplined and they take their jobs carefully. The employees will be highly motivated to perform their best and get the most effective results.

Ambitious

Every employer is looking for ambitious employees. The reason is very simple. Ambition is what makes companies prosperous and flourishing. Employees who act and are willing to take risks are more admired and respected over those who remain passive. There are times when taking risks can be a failure, but they are more likely to bring success to the company and its expansion while inventing new ideas. Inactive and lazy employees will not make a business successful, but enthusiastic employees will. The most ambitious employees will be more dedicated to obtaining an increase in rank, and also aid the company in reaching their objectives. They have a strong desire to grow in their profession. It's true that ambition is the catalyst for creative thinking as well as determination and a willingness to learn - every one of them beneficial for the business.

Intelligence -

We are all aware that being smart makes life easier and intelligent people are generally admired. Being intelligent is beneficial in the professional world. Intelligence is a crucial factor in the world of business and is a strong base to be successful. It is true that there are many variables in the hiring process however, intelligence is essential for any reputable company.

The last thing that executives would like to do is spend long hours proofreading work, giving constant instruction and having to deal with increased stress levels. The company's owner as well as your immediate supervisor have their own responsibilities to handle and when they delegate tasks to employees their employees, what they do not want is lots of questions. What they really want is determination and efficiency. Being able to accomplish objectives of the business is vital however, to succeed at work , an employee needs to have a knack for using soft skills, having the ability to connect with coworkers and effectively communicate. Additionally, every company needs smart people who are able to come up with innovative ideas that will help the company expand and flourish.

Confidence

Confidence is a desired quality for workers. It aids in attaining desired outcomes and motivates employees to accept difficult assignments and take on challenges. Most successful companies are confident of their ability to deliver the best product or service. This conviction encourages a culture that is constantly improving and growing the business. They constantly seek out competent and confident employees. A confident worker is typically more inclined and willing to take on risks or opt to the extremes that a hesitant employee would be reluctant to take on. The best business results are achieved by employees who have faith in their capabilities and abilities.

Success in the past having been successful in the past

The most reliable method to determine the potential of future success of an applicant is to gauge the level of success the candidate has achieved in other companies. Interviewers are looking to determine if you achieved your company's goals and if you've achieved more than the expectations set. What are your achievements at the company where you worked? If you have achievements that are notable, ensure you mention them on your resume.

A hard-working person hard-working

There is nothing that can compare to the genuine effort. Employees who are hardworking aren't so easily found nowadays, and, as a result, they're highly useful on the job market. There are individuals who put in the effort for a while but then slow down. In addition, hardworking employees are the basis of a company's performance. Employers are always impressed by the punctual, disciplined and committed employee. Lateness to work or being procrastinating and being late to work will not aid an employee in achieving his goals in career.

Employers will not be happy and could result in the worker being dismissed.

The hardworking employees know that they need to continue their commitment to work in order to be successful. If they succeed and the business prospers as well.

Self-motivated

People who are motivated by their own will know what they want from life, and they move to the next level and go after the opportunity. They are able to overcome challenges as well as obstacles and fatigue. They are confident in themselves and in others as well. These people are persevering and determined. They constantly upgrade their abilities and know-how. In addition, self-motivated employees do not need to be forced to finish their work. They are hard-working and always accomplish great work. Additionally, they are keen to discover new things and strive to achieve more success.

It is important to remember that self-motivated employees get promoted more frequently than other employees and make significantly more money than employees with average salaries.

Passionate -

Employees who are passionate can be extremely beneficial to employees. They enjoy their job and, most of the time, they do not even think about the work they do as such. It's a fact that money will always be an incentive for employees, but those who are happy at work are the ones worth hiring. Employers love a person who is enthusiastic about his job and determined to go beyond what is expected of them.

People who are passionate about their work constantly surpass expectations and will happily take on new tasks. In addition, someone who is enthusiastic about their work is not even aware that you are working and that is a dream fulfilled for every employer. People who are truly passionate about their work, invest much of their time away from working hours in order to develop their skills and abilities and to expand their expertise.

Reliable

It's a fact when an employee is not reliable The consequences can affect the entire company. Unreliable employees could affect the morale and performance of the other employees and, as a result, negative impact on the overall performance of the company. Additionally, employees who are not reliable often perform work to unpredictability and can affect the clients of your business in a negative way. Being trustworthy also means that you show that you are on time for work as well as being helpful to coworkers and adhering to deadlines. A person who is reliable and reliable is more likely of being promoted.

What is the final verdict? Every business needs and wants competent employees. Do not hesitate to provide an example of every situation in which you've proved yourself that you are a reliable and responsible employee. Don't be afraid to discuss the details when you explain. They'd like to hear about it, believe me.

Loyal Loyal

Every employer is looking for loyal employees. You'd expect the same as an employer, wouldn't you? Everyone doesn't want employees who be negative about their bosses and/or the organization they work for. The ideal employee is one who is ready and willing to do all can to help promote the company. What do you think? When I work with you, I will promise that I will do the greatest I possibly can in order to make the company to grow. Sounds like a good idea do you think?

However what do you think this sounds like? I'm here because you're paying me decent wages.

We all think like this from time moment, but this mindset isn't going to help you get the job you want. This won't help you get accepted or even get you a job.

Most employers today realize the fact that asking workers to sign the commitment to remain with them for longer than 5 years, isn't a realistic idea. Loyalty doesn't mean being within the same organization until you're done. It's about being a diligent and responsible employee when you're working for the business.

If you can demonstrate your commitment to doing your job as well as you can in an interview this will allow the interviewer be comfortable. Also, it will help them recognize that you're an outstanding employee and be confident that you will make a great positive asset to the company. Take note of the following phrase: I'm a loyal worker. This could help your career in more ways than you think.

Team player -

The majority of businesses are comprised of teams. Teamwork and effective teamwork are crucial to the an organization's success. Each employee is an integral member of an organisation. If you're part of the context of a group, you're part of a larger group which means that you must work alongside other employees. Someone who is able to significantly contribute to the overall efforts is regarded as an excellent worker. Anyone who has the capacity to work well as an organization will soon become an admired employee within any company.

What is the significance of teamwork today? The word "teamwork" doesn't mean that everyone in the group will be doing the same thing. It's about making use of the talents and strengths of every individual. Teamwork is a way to maximize strengths and when properly managed, it brings out the best of each team member. The individual strengths of each team member can be complemented through the talents of others or the entire team as a whole.

The work of a team is typically linked to numerous benefits The work can be completed faster when there are a lot of individuals involved, relationships among employees improve dramatically and all members of the team are able to benefit from one another's experiences. A teamwork atmosphere creates an environment that encourages loyalty and friendship to the business. This type of workplace encourages employees to do their best and to support each other.

Optimism -

A person who is optimistic is one who anticipates positive outcomes every time it is possible. It's a fact that optimism is the key to the success of. It provides the necessary motivation for achieving our goals, and is a characteristic that all successful employees have. Optimism can also bring the people's lives meaning. Positive thinking can help a person to feel more confident. Furthermore, employees who are optimistic tend to consider their work to be more enjoyable as compared to those who are optimistic. Recent research has shown that those who were optimistic were also the most happy at work, and the reverse was true for pessimists , who complained often.

We must not forget that no one enjoys being with people who are negativist, negative, or discontent. Employees and coworkers prefer those who are happy and who are positive. Happiness and optimism are infectious.

Numerous studies have also revealed that those who are optimistic often have good reasons to be content with their work: they typically have higher earnings than pessimists, and they are promoted more often. Keep in mind that having a positive and positive outlook is likely to be just as important as a great resume when seeking an employment.

Flexible to change

The best employees are capable of adapting to various individuals, cultures and methods of thinking. They have the mental capacity to recognize how to best approach diverse situations and people.

People who are adaptable aren't afraid to tackle difficult tasks, and are highly regarded by their employers and their colleagues. There are many reasons to be thankful in this; the majority of the people who are adaptable believe that anything can be accomplished even if it involves altering the way of working. They're focused on solving problems and they're not at all intimidated by issues.

There are many companies that have teams. To be a successful team player, an employee must be able to adapt. Workers who are able to adjust to the changing environments, are always eager to discover new things and continuously strive to be at their best are often instances the top performers in any company. Apart from being adaptable and a member of a team, patience tolerance and a good social skill are necessary.

Flexible Flexible

Employees who are great are flexible and open. They don't fear changing. They are always willing to learn new techniques, and they are committed to continuous development. Flexible individuals usually possess the capacity to engage in small talk, which is an important thing to have when working with other people. These are employees who can talk about issues like the weather or movies music, current events or sports while speaking to their colleagues.

If you're an executive in your company or a business owner, you may be considering the advantages and disadvantages of hiring flexible employees. One of the most important recent trends that are taking place in the workplace todayis the hiring of flexible workers is rapidly becoming a part of mainstream. Flexible working can make your workplace a attractive place to work in however, the benefits don't stop there. It is essential to consider that flexible employees are more productive than employees of average.

The ability to take initiative

Many employers are extremely impressed by employees who are able to demonstrate initiative. These workers are assertive, and don't hesitate to inquire about what they want. They are ready to offer solutions to problems and do so in a positive manner. They're not afraid to take the responsibility for their mistakes they've made, which is a well-known characteristic. They are open to criticism and make suggestions when they believe it's appropriate.

In the majority of cases they're extremely productive , which is one reason why they are highly regarded by their bosses. People who are prone to take initiative are the ones who take over when the company is confronted by a deadline or situation where a coworker has to go on a short break. A good employee will never be afraid to assume responsibility or assume a more accountable post. The bosses notice when employees are prepared to go beyond their job, and recognize it by rewarding them or offering them significant bonus.

Being honest

There are many talents and attributes that an ideal employee must possess however it doesn't mean anything if he isn't authentic integrity, honesty, and integrity. An honest employee is truthful about his skills and skills. People who aren't honest could make the entire company appear disreputable and even the whole business could be viewed as insincere. It's no surprise that this is a situation that no business manager would want to see to have for their business.

Honest employees, especially when they are within the upper echelons of the business are highly loved and respected. A trustworthy employee adheres to the company's policies and motivates others to follow the same. While some may believe that cheating is profitable an honest employee won't be able to trust his peers or supervisors. If you are planning to make a significant leap in your career and advance in the corporate hierarchy make sure you be honest with your work, so that you are worthy of the respect of your boss and coworkers.

Reviewing Your Skills

The ability to write down your abilities is essential to be successful at any job interview. A large majority of employers claim that the primary reason they don't employ a candidate is due to the fact that the prospective employee is unable to be able to clearly communicate their capabilities. Consider it for some time. This doesn't mean that they didn't have the abilities needed to perform the task. This means they were unable to not communicate their skills and capabilities with confidence.

Spend some time and think about the answers these questions

What are your general abilities?

What are the areas in which you have competence?

What are your work-related capabilities?

What are your personal characteristics that contribute value?

Your talents are what distinguish you?

General skills refer to capabilities like managing negotiations, teaching research, making great presentations and counseling, as well as organizing, etc.

So, what's the most effective way to respond when you are asked about your abilities and skills?

Include at least three abilities that you utilized in your previous job which you think will be valuable for your new job. Next, you should select one area of expertise you think will be the most crucial for the specific job you're applying for. Give the interviewers a short background on the particular capability and tell them the reason why it is crucial for this position. Explain how this ability contributed to your previous company's growth and success, and then explain how you could apply the same method to the company.

Skills that are specific to your job are the skills and talents you're required to be able to demonstrate to do well in your job. These are the capabilities that a person with the same title yours will need to be able to fulfill the essential demands.

Candidates who don't ask inquiries are making biggest error that could happen. Such behavior can cause the hiring manager and interviewer to loose trust in the candidate. It is impossible to make an impression at an interview without asking minimum of three or two well-thought questions.

The reality is that many employers agree in this regard; and applicants who inquire
at the very least, some smart questions won't make it to the top of the list. If a prospective employee isn't able to ask even one question it suggests that he believes that this job is not important and unimportant. A candidate could appear to

be frightened or not smart enough to formulate questions. Interesting and well-thought out questions tell the manager who is hiring you that you're serious about the position and makes you appear confident and confident.

Let's examine some other serious mistakes!

Failures are caused by mistakes that can lead to failure

1. The interviewer arrives not prepared.

2. Do not show any enthusiasm towards the task.

3. Inability to comprehend the demands of the job.

4. The appearance of being bored or uninterested when interviewing.

5. Incompletely answering questions and providing answers that are too brief or unclear.

6. Incomplete knowledge of the capabilities and skills.

7. Being shy and overly nervous when you are interviewing.

8. Inability to provide examples of the qualities of the candidate.
9. Critiquing past employers
10. Being unable to accept criticism
11. Not being on time for the interview
12. Over-emphasis on the issue of salary

# Chapter 17: What's the Point of This Job?

> "My experience in retail is extensive, having been an associate manager for one of Zara's retail locations for three years. My experience in fashion retail has been so exciting and I've learned so much, particularly as I've built our team from just two employees to seven. Yet I want to take a more direct management role, and the Store Manager position at Warby Parker would allow me to do so while continuing to work in the retail category that I love. Further, as an amateur artist I love that Warby Parker allows store managers to advise on some of their frame designs. Everything about this role seems like an amazing

In the future you'll get asked why you'd like to do this job. What is it about this job that excites you? We've heard a few bad responses before such as: you like the location and the money or the hours of work. All of these are not enough motives to decide to commit a part of your time working for this particular company.

It is important to convey your passion. Consider the eBay example that was mentioned earlier. This person was passionate over eBay as a business was familiar with the product before, and was enthusiastic about the new possibilities.

To create your own personal story, consider your experiences and consider how your abilities are compatible with the job. Are you hoping to lead the staff, but this job will let you achieve that goal? Have you ever wanted to be an associate in a branch rather than being an individual contributor? Whatever your reason, be certain that it's a good choice. Let's take a look at a solid example of a possible person who's looking to manage the retail store of Warby Parker:

> *"I was responsible for launching an advertising campaign at Company X surrounding a new product in less than a month, with a goal of selling 1,000 units. A critical part of this was leading our remote teams of marketing, sales, and operations from three different time-zones. Since a previous team just like ours had failed because of poor communication a month prior, I knew I had my work cut out*

The candidate did an excellent job in demonstrating they understand the requirements for the job and pointed out the key elements that she was awestruck by and also demonstrated that she was able to accomplish the task based on her previous experiences.

A final point: make sure to match the skills you possess with the abilities which the manager hiring you is searching for. The fact that you are familiar with Photoshop isn't worth the effort unless you're working with it. Do not talk about every financial model you could build if your job requires nothing to have anything to do with finance.

> "I realized that the previous team failed for three reasons: one, an overreliance on email, two, no defined goals, and three, a lack of understanding of the product. To address these areas, I first set up a weekly phone call which worked for all three time-zones so that no group was over-worked or tired. Second, I made sure that our one goal was clear: to develop an advertising campaign which would sell 1,000 units. Third, I made sure that our team was trained by the product team to understand the ins-and-outs of the product, as well as the value that it added to our key group of consumers. Through our weekly phone calls, we established a clear plan that capture the two main value-adds of our product. By developing a clear cut goal and making sure the

BEHAVIORAL INTERVIEW QUESTIONS

A lot of job interviews are now focused on how you behave in specific situations, not your accomplishments that you list on your résumé. These are referred to as interview questions, and they usually begin by asking the candidate "Tell me about a specific time that you ..."

The majority of these questions are categorized into four categories:

Collaboration: "Tell me about a time when you worked as in a group or had to collaborate with a team member you disagreed with or had to follow instead of a leader/etc.

> "As a result, our campaign for the new product really took off. Not only did we launch a YouTube campaign in under 5 weeks, we sold 3,000 units of the product - a huge increase from our goal. I attribute this to both my strong leadership of the team, as well as the team's clear feeling that they were a part of a larger mission."

The leadership: "Tell me about a moment when you were required to take charge of a project or lead an inter-functional team/etc."

Conflict and Failure "Tell me about a time when you had a disagreement with a member of your team or failed to meet your goals/had to give bad news/fire somebody, etc."

Solving problems: "Tell me about a moment in which you devised a novel solution to a challenge or had to use a

> "I'm flattered to say that my colleagues describe me as a patient leader. I'm a very driven person, but I also enjoy teaching others new skills. A few weeks ago I taught a colleague how to use an advanced feature in Excel, and he was so grateful that he told the whole office. It as a small interaction, but it meant so much to him that it made me all the more willing to continue taking the time to share my knowledge with other staff."

limited resource/had to work with limited information in order to make a choice/etc."

(See the Appendix 2 for a complete list of the most frequently asked behavior interview-related questions broken out into the category.)

A manager who is hiring for personal stories that can provide them with an understanding of the way you deal with real-life tough situations, and how you could deal with similar situations in the near future. These kinds of questions will require anecdotes from your work or life experiences which showcase your unique capabilities. Although they can be stressful but there's no reason to be concerned. Utilizing a basic framework - PAR can help you organize and recall your favorite stories.

The PAR FRAMWORK

This framework which is "Problem, Action, Result," will help you effectively communicate the story out the Problem you faced The Action that you did to address it, and the result. These three components are essential when telling stories during interviews. Here's how to utilize an interview framework that includes "Tell me about a moment where you were the leader of the team":

THE PROBLEM

This is the place where you define what you consider to be the "Problem" you needed to resolve as well as the context that you were. This could be a specific issue, problem or obstacle that you had to overcome. Include the urgency of your situation for example, a timetable or crucial obstacle that needs to be dealt with. The entirety of your answer should take approximately 30 seconds to speak loudly.

THE ACTION

Then, discuss your Action that you did. With two or three concise steps, write down the actions you took to solve the particular issue. Be sure to mention the people or teams who you collaborated with, as well as any other issues you were able to overcome. Be sure to focus on the actions you did on your own and what you delegated to ensure the interviewer will have a good impression of the way you behaved. This should take about 2 minutes to speak out loud.

> "I'm a very fast reader, but sometimes I can miss critical details. I've taken steps to ensure that I don't go too quickly through important material, and instead try to focus on retaining material. I still have a long way to go, but I'm aware that this is an area in which I need to improve!"

## THE RESULT

Discuss the outcome. What was the result of your decisions and actions? Your primary goal should be to focus on the positive effects, but it's fine to discuss negative effects as it's possible to mention the lessons you've learned from those mistakes. Make sure you measure your answers in terms of dollars saved or made, sales, etc. It will take you about 30 seconds to speak out loud.

The cherry on top At the very close of the essay, write a sentence or two about the things you've have learned. For instance:

The PAR Worksheet

This is it! Are you ready to create your own stories and putting them into the PAR framework? Download your PAR worksheet here, and then fill it with notes to ensure that your most powerful, memorable stories are prepared to be used in the interviews.

When you complete the worksheet, be aware that you could apply that same "situation" for a variety of questions. For instance for example, the "time you were the leader of a team" instance could also be a great solution for a situation where you "had difficulties motivating someone on in your group". You'll likely only get five to six behavioral questions in each interview, so it's okay to make a second attempt at several of your favorite ones.

For additional mock interview advice take a look at Appendix 3, which contains complete examples of interviews.

Strengths, weaknesses, and OTHER ASKED QUESTIONS

You're likely to be asked some additional "traditional" interviews, however, while they might be classics do not be caught answering the question in a dated manner:

Strengths

> "Actually, I think one of my strengths is not getting frustrated even when I'm pushed to the limit. A few months ago, a colleague handed in a weekly report a day late – his third in as many weeks. It would have been easy for me to yell and get annoyed with him, but instead I took the time to really explain how his lateness impacted my work and my own timeline. I think communication is the only way we can start addressing these shortcomings - and sure enough, he hasn't handed in a

In describing your strengths, try to draw attention to your strongest areas while remaining humble. Avoid statements that are absolute, like declaring "I'm the most effective in my field." You should instead consider an approach that is more relaxed and confident:

Insufficiencies

A lot of candidates become caught up in their flaws. You may also have heard the old-fashioned suggestion to make use of a strength disguised as weakness to answer this question, for example "I do too much," or, "I am so attached to my work that I am unable to let go." Interviewers are fed up with these types of answers and want you to recognize the weaknesses that you're working to overcome. This can show that you're aware and self-critical of yourself. Possible answers include:

Other Questions

Like the questions in the interview for behavioral reasons It is important to be precise when responding to other questions during an interview. Questions that are frequently asked include:

Are you a skilled team player?

What is your least-favorite thing about your current job?

## Conclusion

Being successful in an interview is contingent on a variety of factors and the right preparation can ensure that. The most important thing to do is focus on the first impression you make as this is the way interviewers will perceive you throughout the interview . It is also what they will think of your impression after the interview. The best approach to begin is to start with greetings or a handshake, with smile. Make sure you're dressed to the occasion.

It is essential to be prepared for your interview as well. The interview is when you review your resume and attempt to remember your actions in the past. This will help you with the job you've applied for. It is important to be prepared to go through everything, as you may not be aware of the areas that the interviewer is interested in.

Consider the reasons you think you're an ideal candidate to be hired and then use these factors to pitch your skills in front of the prospective employer. It is important to create strong arguments that you're certain your interviewer will be impressed most about your skills and skills.

Be optimistic. This can help you relax somewhat when you consider how difficult certain interviews may be. Many people walk into interviews nervous since they aren't sure what to expect at final. If you're positive you will be able to face the interviewer confidently, believing that you've got everything you need to receive an offer for employment.

www.ingramcontent.com/pod-product-compliance
Lightning Source LLC
Chambersburg PA
CBHW071838080526
44589CB00012B/1038